Contexts of Suffering

New Heidegger Research

Series Editors:

Gregory Fried, Professor of Philosophy, Boston College, USA

Richard Polt, Professor of Philosophy, Xavier University, USA

The New Heidegger Research series promotes informed and critical dialogue that breaks new philosophical ground by taking into account the full range of Heidegger's thought, as well as the enduring questions raised by his work.

Titles in the Series

After Heidegger?
Edited by Gregory Fried and Richard Polt

Correspondence 1949–1975
Martin Heidegger, Ernst Jünger, translated by Timothy Quinn

Existential Medicine
Edited by Kevin Aho

Heidegger and Jewish Thought
Edited by Micha Brumlik and Elad Lapidot

Heidegger and the Environment
Casey Rentmeester

Heidegger and the Global Age
Edited by Antonio Cerella and Louiza Odysseos

Heidegger Becoming Phenomenological: Preferring Dilthey to Husserl, 1916–1925
Robert C. Schaff

Heidegger in Russia and Eastern Europe
Edited by Jeff Love

Heidegger's Gods: An Ecofeminist Perspective
Susanne Claxton

Making Sense of Heidegger
Thomas Sheehan

Proto-Phenomenology and the Nature of Language
Lawrence J. Hatab

Heidegger in the Islamicate World
Edited by Kata Moser, Urs Gösken and Josh Michael Hayes

Time and Trauma: Thinking Through Heidegger in the Thirties
Richard Polt

Contexts of Suffering: A Heideggerian Approach to Psychopathology
Kevin Aho

Contexts of Suffering

*A Heideggerian Approach
to Psychopathology*

Kevin Aho

ROWMAN &
LITTLEFIELD
──────────INTERNATIONAL
London • New York

Published by Rowman & Littlefield International, Ltd.
6 Tinworth Street, London SE11 5AL
www.rowmaninternational.com

Rowman & Littlefield International, Ltd. is an affiliate of
Rowman & Littlefield
4501 Forbes Boulevard, Suite 200, Lanham, Maryland 20706, USA
With additional offices in Boulder, New York, Toronto (Canada), and London (UK)
www.rowman.com

British Library Cataloguing in Publication Information
A catalogue record for this book is available from the British Library

ISBN: HB 978-1-78661-187-1
ISBN: PB 978-1-78661-188-8

Library of Congress Cataloging-in-Publication Data Available

ISBN: 978-1-78661-187-1 (cloth : alk. paper)
ISBN: 978-1-78661-188-8 (pbk : alk. paper)
ISBN: 978-1-78661-189-5 (electronic)

♾™ The paper used in this publication meets the minimum requirements of American
National Standard for Information Sciences Permanence of Paper for Printed Library
Materials, ANSI/NISO Z39.48-1992.

Contents

Acknowledgments

This project could not have been completed without the support from my colleagues at Florida Gulf Coast University, including Mo Al-Hakim, Carolyn Culbertson, Julia Frank, Bob Gregerson, Miles Hentrup, Joanne Muller, Rebecca Totaro, and Glenn Whitehouse. I am especially thankful to my parents, Jim and Margaret Aho, and my teacher Charles Guignon, who read, edited, and commented on the manuscript in its various stages of development. I am indebted to Frankie Mace, Rebecca Anastasi, and the rest of the excellent editorial staff at Rowman and Littlefield International, and to Richard Polt and Greg Fried, series editors of the New Heidegger Research Series, for supporting this project. I would also like to express my gratitude to the following publishers for permission to reprint portions of the following articles and chapters.

"Affectivity and Its Disorders," *Oxford Handbook of Phenomenological Psychopathology*, G. Stanghellini, M. Broome, P. Fusar-Poli, A. Raballo, R. Rosfort, and A. Fernandez (eds.). Oxford University Press. doi. 10.1093/oxfordhb/9780198803157.013.51, 2018.

"Depression and Embodiment: Phenomenological Reflections on Motility, Affectivity, and Transcendence," *Medicine, Healthcare, and Philosophy*, vol. 16(4), pp. 55–63, 2014.

"A Hermeneutics of the Body and Place in Health and Illness," *Place, Space, and Hermeneutics*, B. Janz (ed.). Dordrecht: Springer, pp. 115–126, 2017.

"Guignon on Self-Surrender and Homelessness in Dostoevsky and Heidegger," *Horizons of Authenticity in Existentialism, Phenomenology, and Moral Psychology*, M. Altman and H. Pedersen (eds.). Dordrecht: Springer, pp. 63–74, 2014.

"Heidegger, Ontological Death, and the Healing Professions," *Medicine, Healthcare, and Philosophy*, vol. 19(1), pp. 751–759, 2016.

"Medicalized Psychiatry and the Talking Cure: A Hermeneutic Intervention," with Charles Guignon, *Human Studies: A Journal of Philosophy and the Social Sciences*, vol. 34(3), pp. 293–308, 2011.

"Medicalizing Mental Health: A Phenomenological Alternative," *Journal of Medical Humanities*, vol. 29(4), pp. 243–259, 2008.

"The Psychopathology of American Shyness: A Hermeneutic Reading," *Journal for the Theory of Social Behavior*, vol. 40(4), pp. 190–206, 2010.

"Temporal Experience in Anxiety: Embodiment, Selfhood, and the Collapse of Meaning," *Phenomenology and the Cognitive Sciences*, doi.org/10.1007/s11097-018-9559-x, 2018.

"Neurasthenia Revisited: On Medically Unexplained Syndromes and the Value of Hermeneutic Medicine," *Journal of Applied Hermeneutics*, doi.org/10.11575/jah.v0i0.53334.g40666, 2018.

"Notes from a Heart Attack: A Phenomenology of an Altered Body," *Phenomenology of a Broken Body*, E. Dahl, C. Falke. and E. Erikson (eds.). London: Routledge, pp. 188–201, 2018.

For fruitful conversations and writings that have helped to sharpen many of the ideas in this book, I am thankful to Havi Carel, Anthony Fernandez, Kirsten Jacobson, Drew Leder, Mo Mandic, MaryCatherine McDonald, Nicole Piemonte, Matthew Ratcliffe, Phil Sinaikin, Jenny Slatman, Robert Stolorow, Fredrik Sveneaus, Dylan Trigg, and Kristin Zeiler. I am also indebted to the faculty and students at the Institute for the Medical Humanities at the University of Texas Medical Branch, where I spent a sabbatical as a visiting scholar in the fall of 2014, and to Suzanne Dickerson and Roxanne Vandermause for inviting me to share my research at the Institute for Hermeneutic Phenomenology at the University of Buffalo's College of Nursing in the summers of 2018 and 2019.

Finally, I have an inexpressible debt of gratitude to my partner, Jane Kayser, whose support, tenderness, and love have been unwavering. This book is dedicated to her.

Abbreviations

Works by Heidegger

"GA" indicates the volume of the *Gesamtausgabe* (*Collected Works*). Frankfurt am Main: Vittorio Klostermann. Where available, the lecture/publication date follows the German title. Unless otherwise indicated, all references are from the English translation and pagination.

BP   *Die Grundprobleme der Phänomenologie*. 1927. (GA 24). *The Basic Problems of Phenomenology*. Translated by Albert Hofstadter. Bloomington: Indiana University Press, 1982.

BT   *Sein und Zeit*. 1927. (GA 2). *Being and Time*. Translated by John Macquarrie and Edward Robinson. New York: Harper and Row, 1978. German pagination.

CP   *Beiträge zur Philosophie (Vom Ereignis)*. 1936–1938. (GA 65). *Contributions to Philosophy (From Enowning)*. Translated by Parvis Emad and Kenneth Maly. Bloomington: Indiana University Press, 1999.

CT   *Der Begriff der Zeit*. 1924. (GA 64). *The Concept of Time*. Translated by William McNeill. Oxford: Blackwell, 1992.

EG   "Der Satz vom Grund." 1928. (GA 9). "On the Essence of Ground." In *Pathmarks*. Translated by William McNeill. Cambridge: Cambridge University Press, 1998

FCM   *Die Grundbegriffe der Metaphysik: Welt, Endlichkeit, Einsamkeit*. 1929–1930. (GA 29/30). *Fundamental Concepts of Metaphysics: World, Finitude, Solitude*. Translated by William

McNeill and Nicholas Walker. Bloomington: Indiana University Press, 1995.

HCT   *Prolegomena zur Geschichte des Zeitbegriffs.* 1925. (GA 20). *History of the Concept of Time: Prolegomena.* Translated by Theodore Kisiel. Bloomington: Indiana University Press, 1985.

LH   "Brief über den Humanismus." 1947. (GA 9). "Letter on Humanism." In *Basic Writings.* Translated by Frank Capuzzi and J. Glenn Gray. New York: HarperCollins 1993.

LW   *"Mein liebes Seelchen!" Briefe Martin Heideggers an seine Frau Elfride 1915-1970. Martin Heidegger, Letters to his Wife: 1915-1970.* Translated by Rupert Glasgow. Cambridge: Polity, 2008.

MFL   *Metaphysische Anfangsgründe der Logik im Ausgang von Leibniz.* 1928. (GA 26). *Metaphysical Foundations of Logic.* Translated by Michael Heim. Bloomington: Indiana University Press, 1984.

MSC   "700 Jahre Messkirch." 1961. (GA 16). "Messkirch's Seventh Centennial." Translated by Thomas Sheehen. *Listening: Journal of Religion and Culture* 8(1-3): 40–57, 1973.

N   *Der Wille zur Macht als Kunst.* 1936–1937. (GA 6). "The Will to Power as Art." In *Nietzsche Vol. 1.* Translated by David F. Krell. New York: Harper and Row, 1979.

OWA   "Der Ursprung des Kunstwerkes." 1935. (GA 5). "The Origin of the Work of Art. In *Basic Writings.* Translated by Albert Hofstadter. New York: HarperCollins, 1993.

PS   *Platon: Sophistes.* 1924–1925. (GA 19). *Plato's Sophist.* Translated by Richard Rojcewicz and André Schuwer. Bloomington: Indiana University Press, 2003.

TT   "Das Ding." 1951. (GA 7). "The Thing." In *Poetry, Language, Thought.* Translated by Albert Hofstadter. New York: Harper and Row, 1971.

ZS1   *Zollikoner Seminare: Protokolle—Gespräche—Briefe.* 1959–1971. (GA 89). *Zollikon Seminars: Protocols—Conversations—Letters.* Translated by Franz Mayr and Richard Askey. Evanston, IL: Northwestern University Press, 2001.

ZS2   *Zollikoner Seminare (Abteilung: Hinweise und Aufzeichnungen).* 1959–1969. (GA 89). Edited by Peter Trawny. Frankfurt: Vittorio Klosterman, 2018.

Introduction

Heidegger and Psychiatry

Modern psychiatry is in crisis. Despite all the pharmaceutical and therapeutic breakthroughs in recent decades, Americans by almost every measure are more unhappy and dissatisfied with their lives than ever, and rates of depression and anxiety continue to climb. Among the many concerns are persistent questions about the medical legitimacy of psychiatric diagnoses due to a failure to identify any direct organic cause for the vast majority of disorders, undermining the long-held assumption that mental illness is the result of "chemical imbalances" in the brain. There are suspicions of emerging conflicts of interest in psychiatry's cozy relationship with the pharmaceutical industry, with its ubiquitous presence at professional meetings and its industry-sponsored research and grant funding. There is also concern about the bloated size and dehumanizing taxonomy of the *Diagnostic and Statistical Manual of Mental Disorders* (DSM), now in its fifth edition with more than 365 different illnesses, making it possible to medicalize almost every shade of human suffering, from caffeine withdrawal to shyness to grief. And there is psychiatry's alarming colonization of pediatric health and the growing practice of "polypharmacy," whereby children, some as young as two years old, are being diagnosed and prescribed powerful psychiatric cocktails for multiple disorders, even though there has not been one published study on the effects of these medications on developing brains.

These trends have emerged against the backdrop of an increasingly narrow and reductive paradigm that now dominates the American Psychiatric Association (APA) in terms of teaching, funding, and research, a biologically based approach that focuses almost exclusively on the use of medications to affect changes in brain chemistry. The fact that biological psychiatry invariably pulls human beings out of their relational contexts and reduces them to neurotransmitters has prompted many prominent psychiatrists to rebel against their own profession. Arguably the most famous example of professional defection was psychiatrist Loren Mosher, former chief at the National Institute of Mental Health (NIMH), who publicly resigned from the APA in 1998. In his resignation letter, he writes:

> After nearly three decades as a member it is with a mixture of pleasure and disappointment that I submit this letter of resignation from the American Psychiatric Association (APA). The major reason for this action is my belief that I am actually resigning from the American Psychopharmacological Association. Luckily, the organization's true identity requires no change in acronym . . .
>
> . . .
>
> At this point in history, in my view, psychiatry has been almost completely bought out by the drug companies. The APA could not exist without the pharmaceutical company support of meetings, symposia, workshops, journal advertising, grand rounds luncheons, unrestricted educational grants etc. etc. Psychiatrists have become the minions of drug company promotions . . .
>
> . . .
>
> These psychopharmacological limitations on our abilities to be complete physicians also limit our intellectual horizon. No longer do we seek to understand whole persons in their social contexts rather we are there to realign our patients' neurotransmitters. The problem is that it is very difficult to have a relationship with a neurotransmitter whatever its configuration. (cited in Sinaikin 2010, 244–45)

Contexts of Suffering draws on the existential and hermeneutic phenomenology of Martin Heidegger (1889–1976) to address the very concerns that prompted Mosher's resignation. Heidegger's analysis of human existence (or Dasein) not only dismantles the ontological assumptions inherent in biological psychiatry; it brings the whole person and their irreducible social contexts back into the therapeutic encounter. Heidegger makes it clear that the human being is, first and foremost, not a biochemical object or organism but a situated, self-interpreting activity or *way of being*. In order to understand the experience of psychopathology, according to this view, we have to start from our relation to the world and how this relation is disrupted and breaks down in episodes of mental illness. This gives the psychiatrist insight into the first-person experience of the patient and discloses the extent to which these experiences are already embedded in contexts of meaning. Situating or contextualizing mental illness in this way allows the psychiatrist to temporarily suspend the detached third-person perspective of biomedicine and attend to the experience itself and the ways in which the patient feels, understands, and makes sense of their suffering.

Much has been written on the impact that Heidegger's thought has had on the theoretical foundations of psychiatry, and his own relationship with the profession is rich and enduring. There was, of course, the decades-long friendship he had with psychiatrist and philosopher Karl Jaspers (1883–1969), whose 1919 work *Psychology of Worldviews* and his Kierke-gaard-inspired accounts of "existence" (*Existenz*) and "limit-situation" (*Grenzsituation*) resonated strongly with Heidegger's early project, inspiring them both to form a "fighting alliance" against the rampant scientism that was encroaching into every sphere of German life[1] (Safranski 1998, 127). He also met with and influenced the prominent Swiss psychiatrist Ludwig Binswanger (1881–1966), who introduced a psychiatric approach called "Daseinsanalysis" (*Daseinsanalyse*) that drew on the insights of Heidegger's own "analytic of Dasein" (*Daseinsanalytik*) in *Being and Time* (1927).[2] Against the Freudian ideas of the day that saw mental illness as the mechanistic product of innate drives or unconscious conflicts between the personality structures of the Id, Ego, and Superego, Binswanger argued that mental illness should never be reduced to mechanistic principles because human existence is fundamentally holistic and relational; it is an irreducibly complex interweaving between person and world. Thus, he writes:

> Freud, the natural scientist, or to put it differently, the philosopher of nature, seeks to explain the multiplicity of life by . . . unitary principles. However . . . the human being is not only to be understood as a mechanical necessity. . . . Rather, human existence is understandable only as being-in-the-world, as the projection and disclosure of world—as Heidegger has so powerfully demonstrated. (cited in Frie 1997, 27)

Binswanger understood mental illness, in part, as an experiential constriction or narrowing of the patient's world, and the primary aim of healing is a reopening of that world, a lighting up of new possibilities and relationships through an empathic I-You encounter between psychiatrist and patient. It is the cultivation of these tender and warm connections, so essential for human health, that Binswanger found lacking in Heidegger's cold and impersonal account of "the they" (*das Man*) in *Being and Time*.

Interestingly, Heidegger experienced Daseinsanalysis first hand after suffering a mental breakdown in 1946 after a "de-Nazification committee" stripped him of his professorship at the University of Freiburg and temporarily banned him from teaching due to his Nazi connections.[3] He was admitted to a sanitarium in Badenweiler and treated by Victor Baron von Gebsattel (1883–1976), a psychiatrist trained in Binswanger's school of Daseinsanalysis.[4] Gebsattel's familiarity with existential philosophy, theology, and Heidegger's own work, combined with his therapeutic warmth, had a profound impact on Heidegger's recovery. In a letter from the sanitarium to his wife Elfride he admits, "It was a good decision to come here; for along with the distance from everything connected to Freiburg, the pleasant humanity and spontaneous friendliness of Herr Gebsattel is helping me greatly" (LW, 192; Mitchell 2016, 86). And in 1947, shortly after his release from Gebsattel's care, Heidegger received a letter from another prominent Swiss psychiatrist, Medard Boss (1903–1990), who had read *Being and Time* and thought its account of human existence could help dismantle what he saw as an overly objectifying and mechanistic paradigm in scientific medicine. This letter led to a meeting between the two in 1949 at Heidegger's mountain hut in Totnauberg, where an enduring friendship was formed, leading to a famous decade-long (1959–1969) series of seminars with physicians and psychiatrists in Zollikon, Switzerland.

The *Zollikon Seminars* were initially held at the University of Zurich's psychiatric clinic known as the "Burghölzli," but Heidegger disliked the sterile technological setting of the clinic's new auditorium and requested that they move to the more intimate confines of Boss's home during week-long trips he would take to Zurich every semester (Boss 2001). The seminars represent a watershed moment in psychiatric theory both for its thoroughgoing critique of core assumptions in biomedicine and for its existential and phenomenological interpretations of psychotherapy and mental illness.[5] The central insight of the seminars hinges on the idea that the naturalistic standpoint in medical science neglects a more fundamental question about what it means *to be* human. By reducing human beings to physical organisms determined by causal laws, Heidegger argues psychiatry misinterprets our experience "as something chemical and as something that can be affected by chemical interventions" (ZS1, 155). He makes it clear that the patient is not an encapsulated, causally determined object: he or she is a relational *way of being*, an affective, historically situated, and embodied existence. In order to properly understand mental illness, then, the patient's experience needs to be contextualized in terms of being-in-the-world. This creates an entry for the psychiatrist to see the extent to which our relation to the world and the very the structures that constitute our subjectivity can be disrupted and collapse during episodes of illness. The *Zollikon Seminars* illuminate how this structural collapse alters our experience in different ways, in terms of spatial orientation and bodily movement, in terms of temporal cohesion and unity, in terms of our everyday relations with others, even in terms of our capacity to interpret and make sense of our own suffering.

This kind of contextual attentiveness exposes what is so problematic in American psychiatry today. In his conversations with psychiatrists, Heidegger suggests that no matter how sophisticated our understanding of pharmacology, neuroscience, or molecular genetics becomes, it will be never be able to access the experiential meaning of a person's suffering. This is because human experience is not located inside the brain; it is, instead, bound up in worldly existence itself. The meaning of our experience can be grasped only by attending to our existential situation and the relational structures that constitute it. Yet, it is important to note that Heidegger is not advocating for the wholesale rejection of biomedicine or the pharmacological interventions that come with it. "It is not a matter of hostility toward science as such," he writes, "but a matter of critique regarding the prevailing lack of reflection on itself by science" (ZS1, 95). Heidegger is concerned, rather, with the embrace of scientism in contemporary psychiatry, a kind of uncritical dogmatism that reduces the human being to a neurochemical self. He wants psychiatrists to recognize that "all scientific knowledge is [already] founded as a way of being-in-the-world" (ZS1, 94), that we are already embedded in webs of meaning that are shaping how we experience and understand human suffering.

Contexts of Suffering expands on a rapidly growing body of scholarship that draws on the methods of phenomenology to challenge the assumptions of biological psychiatry and deepen our understanding of the first-person experience and meaning of psychopathology. Figures such as Matthew Broome, Thomas Fuchs, Matthew Ratcliffe, Fredrik Svenaeus, René Rosfort, and Giovanni Stanghellini among others have made significant contributions to this area of research in recent years.[6] What distinguishes the present book from other studies, however, is not only its singular focus on a Heideggerian approach to psychopathology but an explicit engagement with the history of American psychiatry itself and the unique socio-cultural forces that have shaped its development. To this end, there is a sustained examination of the ways in which American psychiatry has created new mental disorders through the manipulation of diagnostic criteria in the DSM; there is analysis of how the pharmaceutical industry has capitalized on the creation of these disorders by developing new medications to treat them; and there is a broad account of the historical upheavals that have shaped the American conception of the self as a masterful individual and how the cultural embrace of individualism has informed our current understanding of mental health and normalcy.

But the primary aim of the book is phenomenological. To this end, it engages the constitutive structures of human experience and illuminates the various ways in which these structures are disrupted and break down in episodes of mental illness. It also examines how these structural disruptions are already enmeshed in a uniquely American life–world and the extent to which this enmeshment colors the way we experience and interpret them. This approach to psychopathology addresses issues of what mental illness means and what it feels like from the perspective of the patient, experiential and qualitative issues that are all too often dismissed when the patient is reduced to the mechanistic firing of neurotransmitters.

CHAPTER OVERVIEW

The book is divided into two parts; the first is phenomenological, the second is hermeneutic. Part I, "Phenomenological Psychopathology," offers an overview of the rise of biological psychiatry in America, the role that the DSM has played in medicalizing the human condition, and introduces the unique contributions of Heidegger's phenomenology and his analysis of Dasein to explore the experiential meanings of mental illness. Chapter 1 establishes Heidegger's critique of biological psychiatry and, drawing largely on *Being and Time* and contemporaneous lecture courses as well as his later *Zollikon Seminars*, introduces the essential structures (or *existentialia*) that are constitutive of Dasein and the ways in which these structures can be disrupted and even collapse altogether in episodes of mental illness. Chapters 2 and 3 explore the experience of this structural disruption from the perspectives of depression and anxiety, respectively, focusing specifically on the structures of embodiment and spatiality, affectivity, temporality, and self-understanding. Chapter 4 expands on this phenomenological analysis by examining these structural disruptions in terms of the loss of one's identity (or being), an "*inability*-to-be" that Heidegger calls "dying" (*Sterben*). The chapter goes on to explore the extent to which biomedical interventions are largely useless in addressing the phenomenon of dying and offers a therapeutic alternative that draws on Heidegger's novel conceptions of authenticity and transcendence in an effort to refashion or recreate a narrative identity in the wake of mental illness.

It is important to note that my account of phenomenological psychopathology does not address major psychotic disorders such as schizophrenia or bipolar depression. It is not because these disorders are not worthy of phenomenological investigations in their own right (cf. Fuchs 2007; Ratcliffe 2017; Sass & Parnas 2007) but because they tend to indicate the presence of a genuine disease of the brain. Although there is still no direct evidence of a chemical imbalance or neurological defect, the fact that patients only respond to a specific class of medications and that symptoms are generally consistent across cultural contexts suggests that these disorders may be different in kind from the more ill-defined nonpsychotic conditions (formerly "neuroses") that have been added to recent editions of the DSM, such as depressive disorders, anxiety disorders, and obsessive-compulsive disorders. One of the central aims of this book is to draw on Heidegger's analysis of Dasein to problematize the phenomenon of medicalization in American psychiatry, that is, of applying a diagnostic label and providing medication for painful and undesirable but often inescapable aspects of the human condition. The ubiquitous neuroses of everyday life tend to fit this pattern; schizophrenia and bipolar disorders do not. From clinical accounts, the symptomology, family history and age of onset, and genetics of psychotic disorders tend to indicate a bona fide medical condition.

Part II of the book, "Hermeneutic Psychiatry," draws on Heidegger's brand of ontological hermeneutics to illuminate the seminal role that "history" (*Geschichte*) plays in shaping our cultural understanding and experience of mental health and illness. By approaching human existence hermeneutically, as a self-interpretative activity that is already suspended in webs of historical meaning, Heidegger's early project not only exposes the limits of biological accounts of mental illness but also provides a framework for the psychiatrist to empathically enter into the patient's world by situating their experience within the relational meanings that constitute it.

Chapter 5 lays out the conceptual groundwork of hermeneutic psychiatry, articulates the core distinction between scientific "explanation" (*Erklärung*) and hermeneutic "understanding" (*Verstehen*), and introduces why it's important for American psychiatry to re-envision itself as an interpretive "human science" (*Geisteswissenschaft*) rather than an applied "natural science" (*Naturwissenschaft*). Chapters 6, 7, and 8 examine the broader meaning-structures of American culture and the ways in which these structures tacitly establish standards of emotional and behavioral normality and how failing to live up to these standards often results in a psychiatric diagnosis. Chapter 6 focuses on the historical conditions that have normalized the American self as a gregarious and assertive extrovert and how this has opened the door for the psychiatric effort to medicalize dispositions like shyness and introversion. Chapter 7 explores the unique history of neurasthenia in American psychiatry to show how turn-of-the-century social upheavals exacerbated our experiences of nervousness, exhaustion, and stress and altered the meaning of the diagnostic terms used to explain them. The chapter goes on examine how the extinct diagnosis has been revived today in the form of functional somatic conditions like fibromyalgia and chronic fatigue syndrome and the extent to which these conditions are already embedded in a context that determines how we experience and make sense of them. The final chapter focuses on the medicalization of rage in the DSM and the distinct confluence of meanings that have informed American conceptions of individualism and authenticity and how these conceptions may be contributing to an epidemic of moral confusion, loneliness, and rage. The aim of these hermeneutic reflections is to show how psychiatry's efforts to medicalize the human condition by applying diagnostic labels to distressing or unwanted feelings and behaviors reveals more about how we interpret and make sense of the self in America today than it does about any chemical imbalance in the brain.

With this said, I want to emphasize that *Contexts of Suffering* is merely offering an approach to psychopathology; it makes no claims to *the* approach. One of the enduring legacies of Heidegger's oeuvre is the recognition that it represents "paths, not works."[7] The metaphor of Heidegger's philosophy as a "path" (*Weg*) suggests it is fundamentally provisional, open-ended, and incomplete, that there are myriad ways to access and interpret what is given in human experience. This book is similarly path-like, offering a phenomenological and hermeneutic analysis of the human situation to provide a tentative entry point into the first-person experience of mental illness and to explore how we understand and make sense of the experience only against the background of a shared historical world. But, as Heidegger says at the end of *Being and Time*, "Whether this is the *only* path or even the right one at all, can be decided only *after one has gone along it*" (BT, 437, translation modified).

NOTES

1. Heidegger wrote a lengthy review of Jasper's *Psychologie der Weltanschauungen* in 1920, and there are numerous references to the text in *Being and Time* as well as references to the concepts of "*Existenz*" and "limit situation." The friendship between the two eventually collapsed when Jaspers confronted the extent of Heidegger's support of Nazism in 1933. Jaspers himself was banished from teaching and research at the University of Heidelberg in 1937 because of his marriage to Gertrud Mayer, who was Jewish (Safranski 1998, 339).

2. It is important not to confuse Binswanger's "Daseinsanalysis" with Heidegger's "existential analytic" (*existenziale Analytik*) or "analytic of Dasein" (*Daseinsanalytik*) in *Being and Time*. Psychiatric Daseinsanalysis is an ontic investigation insofar as it draws on Heidegger's interpretation of Dasein to form general conclusions about individual psychopathologies. Heidegger's project is one of fundamental ontology that is concerned with the question of the meaning of being in general. His existential analytic, then, is not concerned with exploring the affects and behaviors of particular individuals but with the essential structures that make it possible for *anything* to make sense, that is, to come into being in meaningful or intelligible ways (ZS2, 574). This is why Heidegger says, "Daseinsanalysis is ontic. The analytic of Dasein is ontological" (ZS1, 124).

3. Heidegger's ban from teaching lasted until 1949. He was granted the status of ordinary emeritus professor and readmitted to teach at Freiburg in the winter semester of 1950-1951 (Safranski 1998, 390).

4. Heidegger's treatment by Gebsattel at the sanitarium lasted up to six months, not three weeks as Heidegger reported, and it included biomedical interventions in the form of frequent glucose injections that, according to Heidegger, "has a beneficial effect on one's overall health" (LW, 192; Mitchell 2016, 85).

5. The *Zollikon Seminars* constitute volume 89 of Heidegger's "Collected Works" (or *Gesamtausgabe*). There are, however, two different texts that make up this volume. The first text (ZS1), *Zollikoner Seminare: Protokolle—Gespräch—Briefe*, was edited by Medard Boss, published in 1987 by Vittorio Klostermann, translated as *Zollikon Seminars: Protocols—Conversations—Letters* by Franz Mayr and Richard Askay, and published by Northwestern University Press in 2001. The second text (ZS2), *Zollikoner Seminare (Abteilung: Hinweise und Aufzeichnungen)*, was edited by Peter Trawny and published in 2018 by Vittorio Klostermann. This second text overlaps thematically with the first but has extensive additional material, including notes from the early Burghölzli sessions, discussions of "boredom" (*Langeweile*), further commentary on spatiality, temporality and embodiment, discussions of cybernetics and medical technology, new material on the importance of being-in-the-world for psychiatric Daseinsanalysis, and additional seminar notes from July 1964 through March 1966. This text has yet to be translated into English.

6. For a rich and comprehensive account of recent contributions to phenomenological psychopathology, see G. Stangellini, M. Broome, A.V. Fernandez, P. Fusar-Poli, A. Raballo, and R. Rosfort (eds.), *The Oxford Handbook of Phenomenological Psychopathology* (2019).

7. M. Heidegger (1978), *Frühe Schriften* (GA 1), ed. F.-W. von Hermann (Frankfurt am Main: Vittorio Klostermann), 437.

Part One

Phenomenological Psychopathology

Chapter One

Medicalizing Mental Health

A Heideggerian Alternative

THE RISE OF MEDICALIZATION

As the scientific study of mental disorders, psychopathology is primarily concerned with identifying the cause of mental illnesses and establishing diagnostic criteria to classify them and facilitate their treatment. With recent advances in cognitive neuroscience, brain imaging, pharmacology, and molecular genetics, there is growing dependence on biological explanations, which tend to downplay relational and socio-historical factors and interpret etiology largely in terms of genetic predispositions and chemical imbalances of neurotransmitters such as serotonin, norepinephrine, and dopamine. What has taken center stage in terms of teaching, research, and clinical practice, then, is a biologically based approach focusing primarily on pharmaceuticals to affect changes in brain chemistry, resulting in what has been called "medical-model psychiatry," "biological psychiatry," or simply "biopsychiatry." Of course, it is not just scientific breakthroughs that have contributed to the dominance of the medical model. Critics have also pointed to the increasingly close relationship between the pharmaceutical industry and the American Psychiatric Association (APA), highlighting the explosive growth of direct-to-consumer advertising for psychiatric medication, the industry's funding of psychiatric research, and its ubiquitous presence at professional meetings and conferences (cf. Breggin 1994; Kutchins and Kirk 1997; Sinaikin 2010).

The dominance of biopsychiatry today is rather stunning, considering that back in the 1960s and 1970s psychotherapy and psychoanalysis were all the rage. By "psychotherapy," I am referring to any form of treatment of emotional and behavioral problems that primarily use some version of what Sig-

3

mund Freud called "the talking cure."[1] In the broad sense of this word, traditional psychoanalysis and various forms of depth and humanistic psychologies count as psychotherapy, as do group therapy, role-playing therapies, journaling, and other forms of treatment that emphasize the client's self-expression as having a curative effect. At the time, psychotherapy was a ubiquitous presence in popular culture. It appeared in novels such as Philip Roth's *Portnoy's Complaint*, in such plays as Peter Shafer's *Equus*, in television programs such as *The Bob Newhart Show*, and in numerous Woody Allen movies and countless cartoons in *The New Yorker*. It became a running joke that celebrities and the wealthy had spent fortunes and years in any number of different kinds of psychotherapy with little effect. Indeed, by the 1970s, there were over 130 different therapies, each with its own metapsychology and conceptions of technique (Hale 1995, 335; Shorter 1997, 306). As the talking cure turned into a set of disjointed theories, a number of core diagnostic and methodological problems became clear.

In the first place, outcome studies revealed that no therapeutic approach appeared to be superior to any other and that the rates of recovery among those clients treated with psychotherapy usually did not exceed the rate of spontaneous remission of those who were untreated (Horwitz 2002, 196–197). Furthermore, the talking cure was found to be almost completely ineffective in treating serious psychiatric illnesses such as schizophrenia, bipolar disorder, and major depression.[2] This was made clear in a famous 1980s court case involving Rafael Osheroff and the Chestnut Lodge Hospital in Virginia. Osherhoff, a physician who was suffering from major depression, sued the psychoanalytically oriented Chestnut Lodge for malpractice for subjecting him to seven months of intensive, albeit useless, psychoanalysis and denying him access to medication. He eventually was able to transfer to a different hospital, was successfully treated with antidepressants, and was released shortly thereafter.

The *Osherhoff v. Chestnut Lodge* case exposed a growing distrust in the psychiatric community regarding the medical legitimacy of psychoanalysis and created the perception that treating major disorders with the talking cure alone could constitute a form of medical malpractice (Shorter 1997, 309–310; Klerman 1990, 1991). Indeed, it became increasingly evident that the talking cure did not necessarily help patients recover from the illnesses at all. Particularly in cases of psychotic disorders, patients often came out worse than the control group who received no treatment at all (Shorter 1997, 303, 313). Exacerbating this problem from a diagnostic perspective was the inability of psychiatrists to consistently agree in their diagnoses of patients who presented with similar symptoms. Critics often point to the 1949 study by Philip Ash that revealed how three psychiatrists who had examined fifty-two patients in a clinical setting were able to reach the same diagnostic conclusions only 20 percent of the time (Ash 1949; Speigel 2005). Without a set of clear behavioral criteria justifying a given diagnosis, psychiatrists had difficulty in coming to agreement on who was ill and what the ailment was. One psychiatrist might diagnose a patient as a textbook hysteric, while another might diagnose the same patient as a hypochondriac depressive.

The lack of diagnostic precision prompted a dramatic shift in attitudes regarding the scientific validity and efficacy of the traditional Freudian model, culminating in 1980 when the APA published the third edition of the *Diagnostic and Statistical Manual of Mental Disorders* (DSM-III). The importance of the DSM for mental-health professionals in America today cannot be overstated. In the age of managed care, the reference manual is virtually mandatory because insurance companies require a DSM code for reimbursement. DSM-III represented a significant break with earlier versions (DSM-I [1952] and DSM-II [1968]) that were still firmly rooted in in the ideology of psychoanalysis. Spearheaded by psychiatrist Robert Spitzer, this new edition set out to provide a theoretically neutral nosology according to methodological criteria that hearken back to Isaac Newton. Whereas psychoanalysis regarded an individual's behavior as a sign of inner processes or unconscious conflicts that need to be explained in terms of psychoanalytic theory, DSM-III and its successive editions rejected all theory and instead focused strictly on identifying objectively discernable correlations between behavior and diagnosis. As Richard Wyatt, former chief of the Adult Psychiatry Branch at the National Institute of Mental Health (NIMH) put it: "Good psychiatry requires careful observations and descriptions, *unvarnished by theory.*" DSM-III, unlike earlier versions, "attempts to describe things as they are," eliminating the intermingling of interpretation and observation. And this would "add objectivity, reliability, and prognostic validity . . . [by using] the minimal level of inference necessary to characterize the disorder" (Wyatt 1985, 218; cited in Lewis 2006, 4, emphasis added).

In other words, the scientific nature of the new DSM resided in the fact that, like Newton, it makes no hypotheses (*hypothesis non fingo*) about the underlying processes at the root of the disorder. It offers only a "descriptive approach [and] attempts to be neutral with respect to theories of etiology" (cf. APA 1994, xvii–xviii). Given its aim of etiological neutrality, the DSM nonetheless succeeds in constructing a uniquely mechanized and atomistic picture of the human being, where the sufferer comes to be understood as the locus of decontextualized symptoms to be correlated with pre-established diagnostic categories (Cushman 2003; Sinaikin 2010). All empirically unsubstantiated talk of Oedipal complexes, projection, repressed sexuality, sublimation, and so on is rejected. The goal was an objective, ideologically unbiased psychiatry that was not corrupted by the theoretical baggage of the talking cure. Yet, given that biological explanations of mental illness now dominate American psychiatry in terms of research, funding, and clinical practice, the DSM's position of etiological neutrality is a bit misleading

(Horwitz 2002, 132–157; Kaiser 1996). The turn toward more reductive biological explanations should not be surprising if we understand the pretensions of psychiatry to emulate medical science. Such explanations succeed in undermining the long-held suspicion that psychiatry is a "soft" science with little or no medical legitimacy. And recent advances in genetic research, pharmacology, and neuroscience have served to fortify the biological paradigm, resulting in the now all-too-familiar interpretation of mental disorders as chemical imbalances in the brain. As psychiatrist and DSM taskforce member Nancy Andreasen writes:

> The major psychiatric illnesses are diseases....... They should be considered illnesses just as diabetes, heart disease, and cancer are . . . *caused principally by biological factors, and most reside in the brain.* . . . The brain is the organ of the body that serves to monitor and control the rest of the bodily functions, as well as providing the source and storehouse of all psychological functions, such as thoughts, memories, feelings, and personality. *As a scientific discipline, psychiatry seeks to identify the biological factors that cause mental illness.* The model assumes that each different type of illness has a different cause. (1985, 29–30)

US Surgeon General David Satcher echoes Andreasen's sentiment with the authoritative claim that "the bases of mental illness are chemical changes in the brain. . . . There's no longer any justification for the distinction . . . between mind and body or mental and physical illness. Mental illnesses are physical illnesses" (cited in Stossel 2015, 179). The upshot of this view is that mental disorders come to be regarded on the medical model as analogues to physical disease located "in the individual" with a clearly defined "internal pathology that causes the symptomatic behaviors" (Kutchins and Kirk 1997, 31). And, thus like diabetes or heart disease, mental illnesses may require a lifetime of medication for the maintenance of health and the prevention of relapse.

There is, in principle, nothing wrong with medical model psychiatry. The problem from a diagnostic perspective is that it may only be suitable for psychotic disorders such as schizophrenia or bipolar disorder (cf. APA 2013, 87–154). These illnesses tend to indicate the presence of a disease entity, *not* because of any direct evidence of a chemical imbalance or neurological defect in the brain but rather because patients tend to respond positively only to a specific class of medication such as clozapine or lithium and because the symptoms—including delusions, hallucinations, disorganized thinking, and grossly abnormal motor behavior (including catatonia)—generally resemble each other across different social and cultural contexts (Horwitz 2002, 190). On the other hand, the long list of nonpsychotic disorders (formerly referred to as "neuroses") in the DSM vary widely on the basis of context, and the class of drugs prescribed to treat them—often antidepressants or antianxiety medications—are not disorder-specific at all. They are used with mixed results to treat a wide array of conditions, including panic anxiety, phobias, insomnia, obsessive-compulsive disorders, and, of course, depressive disorders (Horwitz 2002, 191; Healy 2006).

Indeed, because there is no direct biological or neurological evidence, these disorders are equated solely with symptoms. Thus, if a patient exhibits the proper number of symptoms over the appropriate period of time, the patient *has* the disorder, even though the organic cause of the symptoms is completely unknown (Kaiser 1996). Even more problematic is how the architects of the DSM have *created* disorders as they try to carve up and isolate the manifold expressions of mental suffering, resulting in the increasingly bloated size of the DSM (Kutchins and Kirk 1997; Horwitz 2002; Szasz 2007; Conrad 2007). The DSM-I, for example, was only 130 pages long, with 106 different disorders, whereas the DSM-V is nearly one thousand pages long, with 365 different disorders, including such nebulous conditions as hoarding disorder (APA 2013, 247), caffeine and cannabis withdrawal disorder (506, 509), binge-eating disorder (350), and disinhibited social engagement disorder (268). Paul McHugh (1999), former psychiatrist-in-chief at Johns Hopkins University, states the obvious when he writes: "Embedded within these hundreds of pages are some categories of disorder that are real; some that are dubious, in the sense that they are more like the normal responses of sensitive people than psychiatric 'entities.' and some that are purely the inventions of their proponents." Arguably the most controversial example of medicalization in DSM-V was the removal of the bereavement exclusion for major depression. In previous editions, clinicians were advised not to diagnose depression in recently bereaved individuals, as grief was viewed as a normal and even a healthy response to the loss of a loved one. Critics argued that the removal of the bereavement exclusion undercuts the therapeutic value of grieving, medicalizing a human response to loss and resulting in the unnecessary over-prescription of antidepressants (cf. Gallagher 2018).

The wave of medicalization has penetrated significant portions of everyday life. Today, for example, nearly half of all Americans could have a diagnosable mental disorder at any given time (Rosenberg 2013). Those who have trouble sleeping have insomnia, those who are excessively shy and introverted have social phobia, those who experience background nervousness at work have generalized anxiety disorder, those who yell at their fellow drivers when stuck in slow-moving traffic have intermittent explosive disorder, those who cannot remain faithful to their spouses have hypersexual disorder, those who are restless and unable to focus have attention deficit hyperactivity disorder, and so on. Indeed, with the number of disorders growing and the spectrum of symptoms broadening, not only are more people being diagnosed with disorders requiring psychiatric medications; they are being diagnosed with multiple disorders requiring multiple medications. Psychiatrist Phil Sinaikin offers an example of "polypharmacy" (prescribing more than one psychiatric medication at a time) from his own clinical practice when a thirty-six-year-old patient came to him for an appointment because he needed refills, and his own psychiatrist was unavailable. The patient was taking a total of sixteen psychiatric medications a day, including: Tofranil (an antidepressant), 50 mg. three times a day; Keppra (an anticonvulsant being used as a mood stabilizer), 500 mg. twice a day; Inderal (a blood pressure pill being used to treat anxiety), 10 mg. three times a day; Wellbutrin (an antidepressant), 150 mg. once a day; Abilify (an antipsychotic also approved for bipolar I disorder), 15 mg. once a day; Eskalith (a form of lithium, a mood stabilizer), 450 mg. twice a day; Klonopin (a tranquilizer), 0.5 mg. twice a day; and Adderall (an amphetamine used for attention deficit disorder), 20 mg. twice a day. What was especially disturbing to Sinaikin is that after interviewing the patient and carefully reviewing his medical history, he concluded that, besides the emotional blow of a failed marriage and the stress of an overly controlling mother, there was nothing wrong with him psychiatrically (Sinaikin 2010, 1–6).

This pattern is perhaps most alarming in the area of child psychiatry. Today, for instance, 12 percent of American children have been diagnosed with attention deficit hyperactivity disorder, and there has been a forty-fold increase in childhood bipolar disorder diagnoses. Indeed, a full quarter of all children and teenagers are taking psychiatric drugs regularly (Khullar 2018). And with the rise of polypharmacy, children are no longer taking a single drug to treat an emotional or behavioral problem but rather pharmaceutical "cocktails" of powerful and sometimes dangerous medications to treat a complex array of problems (Harris 2006). A recent study revealed that over 1.6 million children and teenagers were given cocktails of at least two psychiatric medications, and more than 160,000 children were given *at least* four medications together. A child, for instance, might take the stimulant Ritalin for better concentration at school, the powerful anticonvulsive drug Depakote to control mood swings, the hypnotic Ambien to induce sleep, and the antipsychotic Risperdal to manage anger (Benedict 2006). In a creepy testament to biopsychiatry's colonization of pediatric health, Johnson & Johnson, the company that manufactures this powerful antipsychotic drug, uses LEGO blocks stamped with the word "Risperdal" for children to play with in the psychiatrist's waiting room. It's no wonder, then, that between 2000 and 2007, antipsychotic drug use doubled for privately insured two- to five-year-olds, with only 40 percent receiving a proper mental health assessment. Add to this the frustration for parents who are often told that because these are biological conditions, their children will need some form of psychiatric cocktail for the rest of their lives, even though there have been *no studies* on the effects of psychiatric medication on the developing brains of children (van der Kolk 2014, 228).

Again, the core problem from the perspective of medical science is that there is no direct evidence that mental illnesses are, in fact, medical conditions. Thus, biopsychiatry's claims of scientific validity are highly dubious. Unlike other branches of medicine, psychiatry cannot point to anything biological in the patient that causes the abnormal behavior or emotional distress.[3] Although this may change with advances in neuroimaging technologies, molecular genetics, and brain anatomy research, as of now, the lack of clear biological markers makes it impossible for a psychiatrist to demonstrate the presence of a disease entity. It is probably true that mental illness has something to do with neurochemistry, but cognitive scientists and research psychiatrists have no idea how. The medical model, at least as of now, has not solved what philosophers of mind call "the hard problem of consciousness" (Chalmers 1996). This is because the model rests on *the wholly unproven assumption* that the cognitions, perceptions, and affects that constitute subjective experience are somehow the result of billions of interconnected neurons firing off electrical impulses. And even if neuroimaging technologies were able to clearly demonstrate low levels of serotonin in the brain, for instance, these images fail to explain whether this deficiency is the result of the disease or the cause of the disease. Is the patient depressed, in other words, because he or she has low levels of serotonin, or does the patient have low levels of serotonin because he or she is depressed (Davis 2008, 27)?

A second concern for critics has been the way in which the medical model maps onto the expectations of managed care that emphasize the efficiency, speed, and cost effectiveness of pharmaceutical treatments over more substantive, long-term therapy. Indeed, with insurance providers imposing strict limits on the number of therapy sessions allowed for patients because of their expense, pills have become the norm, with psychiatrists being replaced by primary care physicians who have little or no formal training in mental health (Conrad 2007; Cushman and Gilford 2000). And those psychiatrists that are still practicing are rarely offering the forty-five-minute sessions of therapy once or twice a week for each patient, a practice that used to be standard. In order to survive in the age of managed care, they are now filling their days with an assembly-line form of treatment, offering accelerated twelve- to fifteen-minute sessions of up to twenty patients per day, just enough time to ask about medications and prescription adjustments. The deeper questions regarding the contextual crises and the underlying life-story of the patient remain largely unexplored. As one psychiatrist lamented, "I miss the mystery and intrigue of psychotherapy. Now I feel like a good Volkswagen mechanic" (Harris 2006).

Finally, critics have pointed to the controversial relationship between psychiatry and the pharmaceutical industry. When the Food and Drug Administration (FDA) published *Guidance to Industry: Consumer Directed Broadcast Advertising* in 1997 permitting direct-to-consumer advertisements for medications on television and radio, it became much easier to promote both the diagnoses and the medications that treat them (Mogull 2008). As medical sociologist Peter Conrad writes, "the common tagline: 'Ask your doctor if [Viagra, Paxil, Zoloft, etc.] is right for you,' reflects the new relation among pharmaceutical manufacturers, consumers, and physicians" (2007, 154). The result is a drug-related marketing explosion, with many psychiatrists serving as "key opinion leaders" with financial ties to drug companies (Elliott 2010). This creates obvious conflicts of interest by the very people who create the diagnostic criteria in the DSM. Science journalist Shankar Vedantum (2006) describes the extent of the problem:

> Every psychiatric expert involved in writing the standard diagnostic criteria for disorder [in the DSM-IV] such as depression and schizophrenia has had financial ties to drug companies that sell medications for those illnesses . . . of the 170 experts in all who contributed to the manual that defines disorders from personality to drug addiction, more than half had such ties, including 100 percent of the experts who served on work groups on mood disorders and psychotic disorders.

With American psychiatry's complicity in the medicalization of the human condition, its problematic alliance with Big Pharma, its failure to identify any biological evidence for the vast majority of mental disorders, and its reliance on the dehumanizing nosology of the DSM, many psychiatrists have become increasingly self-critical about the scientific credibility, therapeutic efficacy, and moral standing of their chosen profession (e.g., Blazer 2005; Bracken and Thomas 2005; Breggin 1994; Glenmullen 2001; Healy 2006; Lewis 2006; Sinaikin 2010).

These important criticisms aside, the aim of this book is not to dismiss the biological or genetic aspects of mental illness or, as we will see in later chapters, the value of pharmaceutical treatments. My concern, rather, is that the hegemony of the medical model creates an overly reductive, mechanistic, and decontextualized picture of the self, and, as a result, it invariably fails to engage the complex situated experience of mental illness. I want to suggest that Heidegger's brand of existential and hermeneutic phenomenology is especially valuable in this regard because its primary aim is to dismantle the core ontological assumption of biopsychiatry, namely that the human being is at the most basic level a physical substance of some sort, a self-contained organism no different in kind from other living organisms. On this naturalistic account, everything that exists, including mental phenomena, is reducible to physical substances that can be explained by appealing to the causal laws of nature.

From this starting point, writes Heidegger, "human bodily being (*Leibliche*) is interpreted as something chemical and as something which can be affected by chemical interventions, [and] it is concluded that the chemistry of the physiological is the ground and cause for the psychical in humans" (ZS1, 155). Heidegger's phenomenology aims to suspend or bracket out these naturalistic assumptions in order to attend "to the things themselves." In his words, phenomenology "let[s] that which shows itself be seen in the very way in which it shows itself from itself" (BT, 58). Understood this way, his analysis of human existence (or Dasein) "says nothing about the material content of the thematic object of science but speaks only . . . of *how*, the way in which something is" (HCT, 85). By focusing on *how* phenomena are experientially revealed or given in "concrete" (*konkret*) experience, the phenomenologist is able to access the underlying conditions or structures that constitute our experience. My goal is to show how this method makes it possible to articulate the ways in which mental illness disrupts and modifies these experiential structures and the extent to which these structural disruptions are already embedded in thick contexts of historical meaning. Situating mental illness in this way allows psychiatry to shift its standpoint from the detached, third-person perspective of the medical model to the illness itself, that is, to the first-person perspective of the sufferer. And this opens the way for rich qualitative accounts of *what it means* and *what it feels like* to experience mental illness and points to, what I envision to be, more sensitive and humane approaches to mental health care.

HEIDEGGER'S CONTRIBUTION TO PSYCHOPATHOLOGY

The impact of Heidegger's phenomenology on our current understanding of psychopathology is informed largely through the way in which it undermines the traditional view of mental disorders. DSM-V, for instance, defines a mental disorder as "a syndrome characterized by clinically significant disturbance in an individual's cognition, emotion regulation, or behavior that reflects a dysfunction in . . . underlying mental functioning" (APA 2013, 20). This definition assumes that cognition, perception, and emotion are subjective mental states that (1) reside "inside" the mind or brain of the individual and (2) generate observable evidence through "outer" symptoms or behavior such as speech patterns, posture, movements, affective expressions, or eating and sleeping habits. Heidegger's work has been hugely influential in dismantling this inner/outer view by interpreting human existence not as a substance—a cognizing mind, for instance, or some neurochemical entity—but as the situated activity of being-in-the-world. For Heidegger, Dasein is to be understood not in terms of "*what* we are" but "*how* we are." "So when we designate this entity with the term 'Dasein,'" he writes, "we are expressing not its 'what' (as if it were a table, house or tree) but its being" (BT, 42). He clarifies this with the following:

> Whether [Dasein] "is composed of" of the physical, psychical, and spiritual and how these realities are to be determined is here left completely unques-tioned . . . . What is to be determined is not an outward appearance of this entity but from the outset and throughout *its way to be*, not the what of that of which it is composed but the *how of its being and the characteristics of this how*. (HCT, 154, emphasis added)

Understood this way, Dasein is not an objectively present substance with what-like characteristics (e.g., psychical or material composition; observable behaviors; neuronal or genetic structure) but a unique self-interpreting activ-ity or *way of being* that already dwells in a context of socio-historical mean-ings, that understands how "to be" in this relational context and embodies a tacit care and concern for its being.

When Heidegger employs his method of phenomenology, he begins with first-person descriptions of our own ordinary existence or understanding of being, what he calls "existentiell" (*existenziell*) understanding. "The question of existence never gets straightened out except through existing itself," writes Heidegger. "The understanding of oneself which leads along this way we call existentiell" (BT, 33). But the primary aim of this existentiell inquiry is to identify the essential constitutive structures (or *existentialia*) that make *any* understanding of being possible. This means that human existence and our everyday ability to interpret and make sense of things is structured by "care" (*Sorge*) and made possible by a unitary care-structure. Thus, "the totality of being-in-the-world as a structural whole has revealed itself as care" (BT, 231). For Heidegger, these structures, taken together, constitute the mediating horizon through which things reveal or show themselves in the meaningful and intelligible ways that they do. Identifying how our self-understanding is constituted and structured in this way is important in illumi-nating the subjective experience of psychopathology because it can disclose the extent to which these structures and, consequently, our understanding of being itself can be disrupted and break down in the course of mental illness. We can now turn to a brief overview of how Heidegger envisions our structu-ral constitution and its relation to psychopathology.

Moods

Arguably the most original and influential aspect of Heidegger's contribution to psychopathology is his account of "moods" (*Stimmungen*). This account dissolves the inner/outer distinction by positing how moods disclose the way we are affectively bound up in the world. In *Being and Time*, he explains, "A mood assails us. It comes neither from 'outside' nor from 'inside,' but arises out of being-in-the-world. . . . Having a mood is not related to the psychi-cal . . . and is not itself an inner condition which then reaches forth in an enigmatical way and puts its mark on things and persons" (BT, 137). For Heidegger, moods are not to be understood as discrete sensations or feelings that take place inside of us. As an embodied way of being-in-the-world, there is no distinction between inner and outer because we are already outside of ourselves, situated and entwined in public contexts of meaning. He writes:

> Mood is never merely a way of being determined in our inner being for ourselves. It is above all a way of being attuned, and letting ourselves be attuned, in this or that way in a mood. Mood is precisely the basic way in which we are outside ourselves. But that is the way we are essentially and constantly. (N, 99)

In this view, moods are not fleeting or contingent aspects of human experi-ence. They are, rather, constitutive of what it means to be human, which means we are structurally "mooded" or "attuned" (*stimmungsmässigen*) to the world.[4] He refers to this structure in terms of *Befindlichkeit*, a notoriously difficult word to translate that is sometimes rendered as "affectedness," "at-tunement," or "state of mind" but is perhaps best translated as "situatedness" in the sense that a condition of being human is that we invariably "find" (*finden*) ourselves bound up in worldly situations where things—people, cul-tural practices, natural events, equipment, etc.—affectively "matter" (*ange-hen*) to us in specific ways.[5] We cannot help but find ourselves in moods because we are already woven into a context of meaning that makes particu-lar affective states possible, where, for instance, a thunderstorm can disclose itself *as frightening*, a long lecture *as boring*, or an impending ski trip *as exciting*.

This, however, points to a shortcoming in Heidegger's account insofar that he fails to articulate the nuance and diversity of affective states or, what he calls "modes of situatedness" *(Modi der Befindlichkeit)*. Indeed, in *Being and Time,* he appears to bypass the issue of modes altogether, writing, "The different modes of situatedness and the ways in which they are intercon-nected in their foundations cannot be interpreted within the problematic of the present investigation" (BT, 138, translation modified). This is unfortu-nate because, from the perspective of psychopathology, there are important qualitative and experiential differences between affective states (cf. Ratcliffe 2013). This is especially true when distinguishing emotions from moods. The former are generally regarded as being intentionally specific, that is, they have the character of being "of" or "about" something insofar as they are directed at particular objects, events, and situations in the world. They also have determinate causes and are relatively intense, focused, and short-lived. Moods, on the other hand, are more enduring, diffused, and indeterminate;

they do not have an intentional correlate and are consequently not directed at particular objects but to the world *as a whole*. They are more like atmospheric or global feeling-states to the extent that they both color and open up our perceptual field or horizon of awareness (Stanghellini and Rosfort 2013). Thus, the more inconspicuous, diffused, and atmospheric an affective state is, the more mood-like it is. This explains why Heidegger says: "Moods are not side-effects, but are something which in advance determines our being with one another. It seems as though moods [are] in each case already there . . . like an atmosphere in which we immerse ourselves in each case and which then attunes us through and through" (FCM, 67). When exploring the nature of psychopathology, then, it is important to take care in distinguishing between different kinds of affective states. There is a profound difference, for instance, between a person who is depressed or anxious about something on the one hand, and a person who is *globally* depressed and anxious on the other. In the latter instance, the mood of depression or anxiety constitutes an *a priori* background or horizon on the basis of which an individual can affectively experience or perceive *anything*. Moods, understood this way, are not generalized or diffuse emotions but, rather, serve as the condition for the possibility of emotions, for anything to affectively matter to us in the first place (Fuchs 2013a).[6] As we will see in proceeding chapters, it is often an individual's moods, not his or her emotions, that are illuminated in mental illness.

Embodiment

One way to grasp how Heidegger's notion of *Befindlichkeit* dissolves the inner/outer distinction is to see it in terms of what Matthew Ratcliffe calls "existential feeling," that is, both a "feeling of the body" and a "way of finding oneself in the world" (2008, 2). Like moods, existential feelings are not directed at specific objects or situations in the world but serve, rather, as the background orientation or grip that structures our experience. When we are healthy, this mediating grip remains hidden or concealed from us in the sense that we are not consciously aware of it. A signature aspect of the existential feeling of health, then, is our inconspicuous connection with the world, a taken-for-granted bond that makes it possible to move seamlessly through lived-space, to reach out and handle equipment, engage with others, and perform workaday tasks. In this state, the body is not a conspicuous "corporeal object" (*Körper*) that I am only contingently connected to. It is, rather, a "lived-body" (*Leib*), the living medium through which I engage the world and experience things, and it disappears in the spontaneous performance and flow of these tasks (e.g., Aho and Aho 2008; Gadamer 1996; Leder 1990; Sveneaus 2000).

Heidegger is well known for failing to give an account of an embodied incarnation of Dasein in *Being and Time*, admitting that, "[Dasein's] 'bodily nature' (*Leiblichkeit*) hides a whole problematic of its own, though we shall not treat it here" (BT, 108; cf. Aho 2009). However, in other writings, especially those originating out of the *Zollikon Seminars* (1959–1969), it is evident that Heidegger identifies embodiment as a constitutive structure of human existence. In these seminars, he makes it clear that "all existing, our comportment, is necessarily a bodily (*leiblich*) comportment" and that "bodying-forth (*leiben*) as such belongs to being-in-the-world" (ZS1, 206, 200).

Related to the German words for "life" (*Leben*) and "experience" (*Erlebnis*), the "lived-body" (*Leib*) is not an object that we "have" and that can be viewed from a perspective of methodological detachment. This is why Heidegger claims that the "body-problem (*Leibproblem*) is first and foremost a problem of method" (ZS2, 472). "The lived-body is always *my body*" (ZS2, 409), and my body is not an encapsulated or self-contained object held under the theoretical gaze of a cognizing subject; it is, rather, already bound up and entwined in a practical life-world. This sensual intertwining makes it difficult for me to perceive my body as a discrete object because I am already perceptually situated and oriented in the world on the basis of my body. Thus, "we do not 'have' a body in the way we carry a knife in a sheath. Neither is the body a natural body that merely accompanies us. . . . We do not 'have' a body; rather, we 'are' bodily. . . . We are somebody who is alive" (N, 99). In order to access and understand the qualitative experience of our own bodies, Heidegger makes it clear that psychiatrists should not "confuse our existentiell bodily being (*existenzielles Leiblichsein*) with the corporeality (*Körperhaftigkeit*) of an inanimate, merely present-at-hand object" (ZS1, 233). Prior to any scientific or naturalistic account that explains what I am as a corporeal thing, *I exist* as a situated, affective, and embodied way of being-in-the-world. Thus, "everything we call our bodiliness, down to the last muscle fiber and down to the most hidden molecule of hormones, [already] belongs to existing" (ZS1, 232). My body, from this perspective, is not "here" like a table or chair, occupying a determinate time and place. Unlike *Körper*, my body does not "stop at the skin" (ZS1, 86) because it is already *out there*, stretching beyond the corporeal into a shared world as I move seamlessly through my environment.

But in episodes of mental illness, the mediating activity of the lived-body is often disrupted, resulting in ordinary tasks presenting themselves as difficult if not impossible. First-person accounts of depression, for example, often refer to feelings of being "immobilized," "frozen," "stiffened," and "paralyzed" (Fuchs 2005a; Karp 1996). Pulled out its seamless bond with the world, my body reveals itself as an obstacle or burden, as a clumsy, lethargic, and heavy object. In this state, sufferers describe becoming acutely aware of bodily phenomena that were previously hidden in the flow of everyday life such as constriction in the chest when breathing, a racing heart, nausea, pain in the joints, or pressure and a dull ache in the head (Ratcliffe 2015). In severe cases, the body is described in terms of "depersonalization" or "derealization" as not even belonging to oneself; showing up as "unreal," "alien," or even "dead," as can be the case in panic anxiety, where the sufferer may no longer feel their own body or the sensations of taste, smell, and touch (APA 2013, 214). When we experience our corporeality in this way, lived-space may begin to collapse as perception and sensory motor function and bodily movement become increasingly inhibited and constrained, resulting in slowed speech patterns and postural changes such as bowed head, lowered shoulders, and a sluggish gait (Fuchs 2005a).

Spatiality

From the perspective of our embodied existence, the world is not to be understood as a spatial container. The world, rather, is "that '*wherein*' a factical Dasein as such can be said to 'live'" (BT, 65). When Heidegger refers to Dasein as being-in-the-world, then, he is not referring to an object or thing that resides inside a container. He is referring to our tacit familiarity and involvement with the meaningful setting of our lives. As a situated and involved way of being, I do not occupy space like a corporeal thing. My directional and oriented movements constitute space as the perceptual range or horizon of my experience. Heidegger explains:

> I walk by occupying space. The table does not occupy space in the same way. The human makes space for himself. He allows space to be. An example: When I move, the horizon recedes. The human being moves with a horizon. (ZS1, 16)

On this view, the lived-body is the experiential horizon through which I encounter and handle intra-worldly things, and it "changes constantly through the change in the reach of my sojourn" (ZS1, 87). This embodied orientation makes it possible to grasp things, to bring the things that we are concerned with close to us in our everyday dealings. Heidegger refers to this capacity for bringing things close as "dis-stancing" (*Entfernung*), a term that has nothing to do with measurable distance (BT, 102). From the perspective of embodiment, distance is not a reference to an external geometrical relationship between objects; it is a reference to the everyday familiarity of being-in-the-world. And, although this conception of distance is measurably "inaccurate" (*ungenau*) and "variable" (*schwankend*), it is wholly intelligible within the context of everydayness (BT, 105). This is why Heidegger contends that objective measurability and distance are actually dependent and parasitic on dis-stancing as a structure (or *existentiale*) of Dasein. "Dis-stance . . . is an *existentiale*. . . . Only to the extent that entities are revealed for Dasein in their dis-stancedness (*Entferntheit*) . . . do distances with regard to other things become accessible" (BT, 105, translation modified).

For Heidegger, this means "the body is spacious (*raumhaft*) in the manner of spatial constitution (*Raumkonstitution*)" (ZS2, 426). When I am healthy, the constituting capacity for dis-stancing is open and expansive as I seamlessly bring things into the region of my concerns and engage in the relational practices of everyday life. But in episodes of mental illness, the spatial constitution that I take for granted can break down. When this happens, the structure of dis-stancing is compromised, and the region of my concerns contracts. In these instances, it becomes difficult to handle things, to negotiate with others in social situations, and to perform "in-order-to" (*um-zu*) tasks. The world is no longer navigable, familiar, and home like. It reveals itself as frightening, hostile, and "uncanny" (*unheimlich*). In these states of breakdown, I tend to see myself as helpless, incompetent, and dependent, as someone who is no longer "making space" as the familiar setting of my life but simply occupying space as an alienated corporeal thing.

Relationality

Because we are already involved in a public world, our existence is always relational or intersubjective. This means Dasein is not an isolated, self-contained "I." It is, rather, more like a mass term that captures the way that human existence is shared or communal. Thus, being-in-the-world is always already "being-with-others" (*Mit-dasein*). As a situated and shared way of being, I understand who I am and what matters to me only in relation to my involvement with others. This relational ontology suggests my identity or self-interpretation is indelibly shaped by how others understand and perceive me. Psychopathology, in this regard, often creates a stigmatized identity (cf. Goffman 1963) as agitation, awkward behavior, and inhibited motility, and comportment disrupts the social order and the taken-for-granted flow of daily life. And this disruption is mirrored or reflected back on the suffering individual. The disapproving social judgment of others leaves a stigma or mark that not only exacerbates already diminished cognitive and sensory motor capacities and competencies in handling ordinary situations; it also shapes and constitutes the sufferer's own self-interpretation. This is what Heidegger means when he refers to the "the real dictatorship of the They (*das Man*)," and why he claims that "Dasein, as everyday being-with-one-another, stands in *subjection* (*Botmässigkeit*) to others" (BT, 126). The fact that moods disclose how we find ourselves in a public world illuminates the ways in which others exercise a silent power over us to such an extent that they "supply the answer to the question of *who* [we are]" (BT, 128, my emphasis).

Understanding the self in relational terms fortifies the phenomenological critique of reductionism in biopsychiatry, revealing how psychopathology is not a reference to private mental states located inside the mind or brain of the individual. It is, rather, a public expression of meaning and significance that can disturb the pregiven web of social expectations characteristic of health and normalcy. And this disturbance is often complicated by the fact that the source of suffering is not physically visible to others as it is with other medical conditions. Without a wheelchair, physical lesion, cast, or cane to point to, for example, the suffering individual can be further stigmatized and discredited for acting on the basis of something that is "unreal," "in your head," or worse, a "moral failing" (Aho and Aho 2008, 111–114). This can result in feelings of reflexive shame and guilt and isolating behavior that in turn creates a downward spiral that further undermines mental health (Fuchs 2003).

Temporality

Much has been written on the ways that psychopathology can distort the experience of time. On a physiological level, it can create the experience of "desynchronization" (Fuchs 2006) that disrupts the natural rhythmic equilibrium of the body as it pertains to processes such as sleep and menstrual cycles, digestion, temperature regulation, appetite, and sexual desire, and this can be extended to affective disturbances arising from bodily disunity with seasonal and atmospheric rhythms. On the social level, desynchronization can result in a sense of disconnection from public time as the busy demands of work and interactions with family and friends clash with lethargy and dulled cognitive functioning. References to feeling "overwhelmed," "unable to keep up," and "stressed" by the pace and harried obligations of modern life are common (Levine 1997; 2005). This can result in the erosion of stabilizing relationships and emotional support systems that can exacerbate experiences of isolation and loneliness.

But Heidegger's analysis of Dasein points to a deeper experience of temporal disruption beyond the physiological and social aspects of desynchronization, one that involves the contraction or closing up of existence itself. Heidegger suggests that our ordinary view of time as a linear sequence of "now points" that are external to us (e.g., clock-time) is actually derived from and made possible by what he calls "primordial temporality" (*ursprüngliche Zeitlichkeit*). For Heidegger, this means the traditional philosophical question, "What is time?" is misleading. The more appropriate question is "Who is time" (CT, 22)? The answer is, of course, Dasein itself. Heidegger forwards the idea that human existence *is time* as a horizonal manifold that simultaneously stretches backward into the past and forward into the future. He refers to this manifold structure in terms of "thrown projection" (*geworfen Entwurf*) in the sense that, out of the present, we are *thrown* into a specific situation (the past), our "having-been-ness" (*Gewesenheit*), and it is against the background of this situation that we *project* ourselves into future possibilities. This means that Dasein is both *not yet* (futural) and what it *was* (having-been), that the possibilities we project for ourselves are always mediated by the socio-historical situation into which we have been thrown (BP, 265). This is why, in order to grasp the meaning of human existence, Heidegger stresses the importance of recovering the original sense of the Greek term *Ekstatikon*. Our temporal constitution is ex-static in that we literally "stand" (*stasis*) "outside" (*ex*) ourselves by "running forward" (*vorlaufen*) into the future, into historically situated possibilities that are *not yet*. Thus, "temporality is the original 'outside-of-itself,' the ekstatikon" (BP, 267).

What distinguishes Dasein's existence from that of other animals, then, is that it is constituted by temporality, and the ecstatic unity of this temporalizing framework opens up a disclosive horizon—the "there" (*Da*) of Dasein—on the basis of which entities can reveal themselves *as such*. This is why Heidegger writes, "The ecstatical unity of temporality . . . is the condition for the possibility that there can be an entity which exists as its 'there'" (BT, 350). Mental illness can disrupt this temporal unity and close down the future as a horizon of possibilities. The result is often a feeling of being trapped in the present (Fuchs 2005a). This experience of temporal collapse has been described in terms of the "slowing down," "dragging," or even "stopping" of time (Levine 2005; Ratcliffe 2015), and this makes it difficult for me to understand myself, that is, to project a meaningful purpose or "for-the-sake-of-which" (*das Wormiwillen*) that both constitutes the sense of who I am and holds that identity or self-interpretation together. This disruption points to a final structure of human experience, what Heidegger refers to as "understanding" (*Verstehen*).

Understanding

When ecstatic temporality contracts or closes down, it can strip away one's capacity for self-determination, that is, to interpret and give meaning to one's situation, and this disrupts the experiential structure of understanding. For Heidegger, "to *exist* is essentially . . . to *understand*" (BP, 276, my emphasis), and this prereflective capacity to understand and make sense of things is always anterior to the reductive ontology of biomedicine. This is why he writes:

> The fact that physiology and physiological chemistry can scientifically explain man as an organism is no proof that in this "organic" thing, that is, in the body scientifically explained the essence of man consists. . . . The "essence" of man—lies in its existence. (LH, 228–29)

The claim that existence or understanding is the essence of being human reveals one of the distinctive features of Heidegger's analysis of Dasein. In his view, the self is constituted not by some pregiven nature or substance-like attribute but by an ongoing relational tension between "facticity" (*Faktizität*) on the one hand and "transcendence" (*Transcendenz*) on the other. This tension reveals that humans do not, like other animals, simply act out of instinct or necessity arising out of the facts of our biochemical givenness. I am, rather, a self-making or self-creating being who has the capacity to exist *for myself*, that is, to transcend, to "surpass," or "exceed" (*übersteigen*) my factical nature by interpreting it and giving it meaning. Heidegger explains:

> Dasein is thrown, thoroughly amidst nature through its bodiliness, [but] transcendence lies in the fact that [nature] is surpassed by Dasein. In other words, as transcending, Dasein is beyond nature, although as factical, it remained environed by nature. As transcending, i.e., as free, Dasein is something alien to nature. (MFL, 166)

In this view, I exist or understand who I am only in terms of the meanings that I project for myself by interpreting and making sense of the factical situation that I have been thrown into. Transcendence, then, is not a contingent or accidental property of Dasein. "It is not just one possible comportment (among others) . . . it is the basic constitution of Daesin's being, on the basis of which Dasein can at all relate to beings in the first place" (MFL, 165). This means understanding is constitutive of being a self. "Transcendence," says Heidegger, "*constitutes selfhood*" (EG, 108, my emphasis). But episodes of mental illness can unsettle and disrupt the structure of understanding, eroding away the meaning and significance of my projects and dimming my capacity for self-creation. In these instances, I am often incapable of transcendence because the future is not experienced as an expansive horizon rich with meaningful possibilities that I can press into. It is, rather, a narrow and constricted black hole that is affectively hollowed out, "empty," "negative," or "meaningless" (cf. Karp 1996; Ratcliffe 2015). Indeed, as we will see in the following discussions of depression and anxiety, in severe cases of structural collapse, when understanding is wholly compromised, the very possibility of *being a self* is lost.

This brief overview helps to clarify what is phenomenologically distinctive about mental illness and exposes the limits of medical model psychiatry. A Heideggerian approach to psychopathology reveals that the affective experience and meaning of mental illness does not reside in the physical body, in neurological pathways, or biochemical processes. It is, rather, bound up in the very structures that constitute my existence and involvement in the world. To reduce mental illness to a chemical imbalance or brain disease is to overlook the embodied and situated person who is suffering and the struggle involved in interpreting and making sense of it. My illness means something to me because I am already *out there*, engaged and embedded in webs of meaning, in a common world that shapes in advance how I understand and interpret my suffering. It is "this common world into which every maturing Dasein first grows . . . that governs every interpretation of Dasein" (HCT, 246). Thus, it is not by neurological or cognitive processes but by being-in-the-world that my experience matters to me and feels the way that it does. And, as we turn to phenomenological accounts of depression and anxiety in proceeding chapters, we will begin to see the extent to which our relation to the world can be disrupted and the toll this can take on our ability *to be*, that is, to understand and give meaning to our experience and to our existence as a whole.

NOTES

1. Freud initially referred to what he did as "psychotherapy" (*Psychotherapie*) and later replaced it with the designation "psychoanalysis" (*Psychoanalyse*) and its practitioner as a "psychoanalyst" (*Psychoanalytiker*) (Groth 2019).

2. Freud was well aware of the talking cure's inability to successfully treat psychotic conditions like schizophrenia. In a 1936 letter to Medard Boss, he writes: "It is true that I have seen little success in the analytic treatment of schizophrenia. My advice not to use this method in private practice has practical motives. The failures are written about in accounts of analysis and damage its reputation" (Boss 2019, 177).

3. Indeed, the Surgeon General's report on mental health states: "The precise causes (etiology) of most mental disorders are not known. . . . All too frequently a biological change in the brain (a lesion) is purported to be the 'cause' of a mental disorder, based on finding an association between the lesion and a mental disorder. The fact is that any simply association—or correlation—cannot and does not, by itself, mean causation" (Surgeon General 1999, chapter 2, sec. 5. para. 1, 9).

4. This is why Heidegger says, "The fact that moods can deteriorate and change over time means simply that in every case Daesin always has some mood" (BT, 134).

5. *Befindlichkeit* is derived from *befinden* ("to find *oneself* in a certain state or situation"), as in the ordinary expression "Wie befinden Sie sich?" which means, "How are you?" or more literally, "How do you find (*finden*) yourself?" It has been translated in a number of different ways, for instance, as "state-of-mind," "affectedness" (Dreyfus 1991), "disposition" (Wrathall 2001), and "findingness" (Haugeland 2013). Here, I follow Guignon's (1984) translation as "situatedness" because I feel it best captures the sense of being affectively bound up in a worldly context or situation. For an excellent discussion of the myriad uses and translations of this term, see Elpidourou and Freeman (2015).

6. When we are healthy and going about our everyday lives, this background sense of "mattering" is so close and familiar to us that it withdraws to the extent that we are unaware of our moods. This poses unique challenges for psychologists and psychiatrists because moods are generally disclosed to us prereflectively, that is, "prior to all cognition and volition, and beyond their range of disclosure" (BT, 136). We cannot get behind our moods and examine them from a perspective of detachment and objectivity because this dispassionate perspective is itself a mood. Thus, the best way to gain access to the lived-experience and meaning of psychopathology is not by taking an attitude of methodological detachment but by phenomenology, by attending to first-person descriptions of how the affective and orienting structure of *Befindlichkeit* is disrupted or breaks down.

Chapter Two

Depression

Disruptions of Body, Mood, and Self

Marcia Angell, a prominent physician and former editor of the *New England Journal of Medicine,* penned one of the more influential critiques of bio-psychiatry in a scathing two-part attack published in the *New York Review of Books.*[1] Angell suggests that the media, the pharmaceutical industry, and medical professionals have manufactured a mental health crisis by uncritically accepting the theory that illnesses like depression are caused by chemical imbalances in the brain and that these imbalances can somehow be corrected by means of antidepressants.[2] Needless to say, the response to Angell from the psychiatric community was swift. Well-known psychiatrists such as Peter Kramer, John Oldham, and Daniel Carlat challenged Angell for questioning the status of depression as a biochemical disorder and defended the use of antidepressant medication. Kramer (2011), for example, criticized Angell's reticence in accepting the medical legitimacy of depression and highlighted the long-term efficacy and health-promoting benefits of antidepressants. Oldman (2011) argued that whether or not "chemical imbalances are causes of mental disorders or symptoms of them" is not the point. "The bottom line is that medications often relieve the patient's suffering, and this is why doctors prescribe them." And Carlat (2011) claimed that regardless of the evidence provided by Angell concerning the scientific validity of the chemical imbalance theory, the "unequivocal if perplexing truth about antidepressants—on the whole, [is that] *they work.*" But what was missing in this interesting exchange between physicians was a critical engagement with the experience of depression itself, with people who actually live with depression and take psychiatric medication. These first-person accounts are crucial because they provide a point of entry into depression that is all too often overlooked in

23

quantitative studies and impersonal analyses of efficacy data, statistical indi-
ces, and causal correlations. Indeed, one of the central problems in the ongoing debate about the medical legitimacy of depression is that personal narratives are often dismissed as unscientific and anecdotal. Yet, dismissing these
first-person accounts prevents medical experts and the public in general from
understanding the experience and affective meaning of being depressed.

Although social scientists have been drawing on experiential reports for
years to critique what psychiatrist Peter Breggin (1994) calls the "psycho-
pharmaceutical complex" and to address the various ways in which historical
conditions and socio-economic forces contribute to depression and psychiatric morbidity (e.g., Blackman 2001; Fraser 2001; Kleinman and Good 1985;
Rose 2007), the aim of this chapter is strictly phenomenological. Thus, I am
not trying to offer a sociological critique or attempt to expose various epi-
demiological conditions in America. Instead, I am concerned with how depression reveals or shows itself *on its own terms* without any ontological
assumptions about what the experience actually is. This allows us to draw
some general conclusions about how the depressed individual experiences
the world, moves through lived-space, and expresses and understands who
they are.

MOVEMENT AND LIVED-SPACE

As we saw in chapter 1, approaching mental illness from a phenomenological
perspective helps to shed light on the limits of the neurochemical view of the
self. On this view, the depressed person is reduced to a causally determined
system of neural circuits, where all explanations of behavior and symptomology must "pass through the brain and neurochemistry" (Rose 2003, 57).
Phenomenology exposes the problem with such an account because it fails to
provide any insight into the individual's own feeling or experience. Again,
from a phenomenological perspective, the individual is not to be regarded as
a causally determined "corporeal body" (*Körper*) but as a "lived-body"
(*Leib*), a situated, affective, and embodied *way of being*. This is why Heidegger writes, "Our being embodied is essentially other than merely being en-
cumbered with an organism. Most of what we know from the natural sciences about the body and the way it embodies are specifications based on the
established *misinterpretation* of the body as a mere natural body" (N, 99, my
emphasis). The body, in this view, is not a "mere natural body" (*bloßer
natürlicher Körper*); it is, rather, the mediating horizon on the basis of which
I perceive, feel, interact with others, and make sense of the world. It is not
something I *have*; it is who I *am*.

What is enigmatic about the lived-body from the point of view of mental
health is its hiddenness. When we are healthy and absorbed in the activities

of everyday life, we live through the medium of our own body without explicitly reflecting on it. This means the lived-body remains transparent to us; our arms, legs, and hands, indeed, our corporeality as a whole disappears in the practical flow of our daily lives as we move through world, handling equipment and engaging in social practices. In these ordinary activities, there is no separation between self and world because we are already bound up in the particular situation that we find ourselves in. When I wake up in the morning, for instance, the purposive activities of taking a shower, getting dressed, and making coffee are performed without mental reflection because my body is already habitually geared to these movements and propels me forward. This means that our primary orientation in the world is one of prereflective doing and acting that is anterior to consciousness and the mind-body distinction. Maurice Merleau-Ponty explains this point when he says: "Consciousness is in the first place not a matter of '*I think that*' but of '*I can*'" (1962, 137). And this spontaneous "I can" is constituted and structured by what he calls the "bodily-schema" (*schéma corporel*), a reference to the kinesthetic, sensory-motor grip that we already have on things, allowing us to prereflectively navigate our way through the world. In this way, the bodi-ly-schema both enables and limits our movement, gait, and posture and is always operating inconspicuously in proportion to our various activities and projects.

What is interesting in first-person accounts of depression are the consis-tent references to breakdown of this mediating schema, where the seamless "I can" is replaced with an incapacitating "I can't." These descriptions reveal how the light and fluid synergy between body and world thickens and slows down, and our taken-for-granted ability to stand up and move, to reach out and take hold of things is disrupted. This results in feelings of the world contracting, of space closing in and smothering the depressed person. In his famous memoir, *Darkness Visible*, William Styron describes experiencing "slowed down responses, near paralysis . . . feeling[ing] sapped, drained . . . [and] smothering confinement" (1990, 47, 50). Elizabeth Wurtzel in *Prozac Nation* echoes Styron, writing: "I am trapped in my body as I have never been before. . . . I literally cannot move" (1995, 2). A man in his early thirties describes a sense of doom as his sensory motor functions diminish and the spatial world shrinks, "causing a paralysis. . . . [It] actually paralyzes you" (Karp 1996, 29). A middle-aged woman refers to this sensation in terms of "treading water [and] drowning," and a woman in her late forties describes a "sense of being trapped or being caged," which triggers a "feeling like I'm being smothered in that I can't breathe. I am being suffocated" (Karp 1996, 29). Of course, the more acute the depression, the more complete and totaliz-ing the "I can't" becomes. A middle-aged man writes:

> [W]hen you're really depressed, you know, if you're in your bedroom and
> someone said there's a million dollars on the other side of the room and all you
> have to do is swing your feet over the edge of the bed, and walk over and get
> the million, you couldn't. . . . I mean you literally couldn't. (Karp 1996, 30)

Others describe the collapse of the bodily-schema in term of being physically
crippled and wholly dependent on others. A woman in her early twenties
writes: "What is most terrible about my illness is sometimes having to be
dependent. . . . The illness cripples you. It can really cripple you. It's dis-
abling" (Karp 1996, 31).

These descriptions reveal how the transparent and seamless bond between
body and world is broken and our corporeality obtrudes in its place as something clumsy and heavy, a foreign obstacle or thing that inhibits our practical
engagement with the world (Fuchs 2005c). In this state, the smooth tacit
competence of our everyday practices dissolves, resulting not only in slowed
sensory-motor responses and a diminished ability to move through the world
but also an immobilizing loss of appetite, libido, and drive for things that
used to be pleasurable and fulfilling. A woman in her midthirties writes that

> you name the things to yourself that you used to love to do. Eating! Sex! Even
> reading a book. Going for a walk in the woods. You can't even remember what
> it's like to go and do something and feel pleasure from it. You look at the
> world, the array of things that you could do and they're completely meaning-
> less to you. They're as meaningless to you as if you were an earthworm. . . .
> And you come to this terrible still point where there's no reason to move
> because there's nothing out here for you. (Karp 1996, 32)

This loss of meaning relates to another experiential quality of depression,
namely an inability to be emotionally affected by the world. In depression,
activities and projects that used to mean something no longer move us.
Indeed, one of the cruel ironies in first-person accounts is not the usual
reference to overwhelming feelings of sadness, anger, and grief but rather the
"feeling of *not feeling*" (Fuchs 20005c, 100). In order to understand this
affective lack, we can revisit what Heidegger says about moods.

DEPRESSION AS DEEP BOREDOM

Heidegger's work is especially helpful in exploring the affective dimensions
of depression because he suggests that human existence is shaped not by
what we *know* about the world but by how we *care* about it and our place in it
(BT, 121). Again, an essential structure or condition of being human is what
Heidegger calls, "situatedness" (*Befindlichkeit*), which means we invariably
find ourselves involved in situations that we care about and that matter to us.
As a philosophy professor absorbed in the meanings of the academic world,

for example, my books and computer, my relationship with my students, and my identity as a teacher stand out as mattering to me in a way that is fundamentally different from the way they might matter to someone else. For Heidegger, this means moods cannot be understood as feelings or states of mind that take place *inside* of us. There is no distinction between inner and outer because our emotional lives are always situated in public contexts of meaning and colored with shared significance (BT, 136). Indeed, it is only on the basis of our engagement in contexts of meaning that we can find ourselves in moods—in situations that affect us in particular ways. Moods in this view are always working behind our backs to orient us in the world; they direct us toward things that matter and provide a tacit sense of what counts for is in specific situations. Heidegger's interpretation of mood as a background sense of caring and mattering is helpful in understanding the experience of depression because it reveals how the mood can shape our relationship not just to particular things but to *everything*.

Although Heidegger never thematically engages depression as a mood, his penetrating analysis of "boredom" (*Langeweile*), especially in his 1929/1930 lecture-course *The Fundamental Concepts of Metaphysics*, offers clues into how the depressed person affectively resonates to the world. In making his case, Heidegger distinguishes between ordinary experiences of boredom and what he calls "deep" or "profound boredom" (*tiefe Langeweile*). In ordinary boredom, our experience has the characteristic of an emotion rather than a mood because it is generally directed towards a conspicuous thing or situation. I might, for instance, be bored with a book, a movie, or a lecture. In this case, my boredom has an identifiable object. I am bored *with* such and such (FCM, 128). Heidegger also identifies a deeper and less conspicuous form of boredom. He gives the example of going to a dinner party and getting caught up in the gossip, laughter, and high spirits of the event. It is only later, after returning home, that I realize I was bored the whole time. In this case, I cannot point to anything in particular about the party that was boring because the party as a whole was boring; it just "killed time" (FCM, 112). Heidegger suggests that this second form of boredom is more primordial and mood-like than the first because it is more hidden and diffused, but it is also similar in the sense that it is situational and transient. Once I put the uninteresting book down or leave the party, I am no longer bored. Both of these forms are contrasted with deep or profound boredom.

Profound boredom has the characteristic of a mood because it is not directed at a particular object or situation. Here, "we are *elevated beyond* the *particular situation* and beyond the *specific beings* surrounding us" (FCM, 137). The overwhelming disinterest that one feels in profound boredom signifies that the world *as a whole* is boring, where nothing stands out as significant and meaningful. "In this boredom," writes Heidegger, "nothing appeals to us anymore; everything has as much or as little value as everything else" (MSC, 50–51). In this state of affective flatness, we are unable to qualitatively distinguish any projects, relationships, goals, or identities that matter in our lives because "what is boring is here diffused throughout the particular situation as a whole" (FCM, 128). In this state, boredom "pene-trates us and attunes us through and through . . . [like an] insidious creature that maintains its monstrous essence in our Dasein" (FCM 79). As a woman in her early thirties writes, "Nothing human beings value matters any more . . . [not] music, laughter, love, sex, children, toasted bagels and the *Sunday New York Times*, because nothing and no one can reach the person trapped in the void" (Karp 1996, 24). Elizabeth Wurtzel describes living in a "computer program of total negativity. . . . It involves a complete absence of affect, absence of feeling, absence of interest" (1995, 21). Depression bleach-es out the affective radiance of the world, and this helps us to understand why so many first-person accounts use light and color metaphors to describe the experience. Andrew Solomon writes, "becoming depressed is like going blind, the darkness at first gradual, then all encompassing" (2001, 50). A woman in her midtwenties explains:

> I was depressed the whole time. There wasn't like a let up of a good day or a bad day. In fact, when I look back on all those years I can't even remember events that stick out. It seems all black. (Karp 1996, 33)

A man in his early forties describes his depression in terms of its "unrelieved monochromatic quality" (Karp 1996, 33). Another man in his early thirties says, "It's kind of like a black thought process that just begins to take over" (Karp 1996, 31). And William Styron refers to it as "a grey drizzle of horror" (1990, 50).

Immersed in this monochromatic atmosphere, the affective qualities of our perceptions are diminished and hollowed out. Things that used to be experienced as alive, warm, and beautiful now appear dead. A woman in her early thirties writes:

> I had no pleasure in anything. What finally got me [was that] I looked at the trees turning [colors in the fall] and I didn't care. I couldn't believe it. I'd be looking at this big flaming maple and I'd look at it and I'd think, "there it is, it's a maple tree. It's bright orange and red." And nothing in me was touched. (Karp 1996, 61)

In severe cases, this loss of affectivity can result in delusional experiences of "derealization" or "depersonalization," in which one feels as if they are not actually there and the world is not real (Fuchs 2005a). Writer Susanna Kay-sen explains that in her situation, "reality lost its substance and [became] ghostly, transparent, unbelievable" (2001, 43). William James quotes a de-pressed patient who says, "I see, I hear, but the objects do not reach me, it is as if there were a wall between me and the outer world" (cited in Ratcliffe and Broome 2012, 367). Dutch psychiatrist Piet Kuiper offers his own account of derealization in describing the unreality of his own wife.

> Someone who resembled my wife was walking beside me, and my friends visited me. . . . Everything was as it would be normally. The figure representing my wife constantly reminded me of what I had failed to do for her. . . . What looks like a normal life is not. (cited in Fuchs 2005a, 113)

These delusions can result in the perception that one's own body is lifeless and unreal. Writer Darcey Stenke says "My body began to feel as dull and dead as the bookshelf or the hardwood floor" (2001, 63). Another writer, Joshua Shenk, refers to his lack of feeling in terms of it being "the emotional equivalent of a dislocated limb" (2001, 248–49).[3]

These first-person accounts point to depression as an experience of profound and totalizing disconnection. They also provide some insight into the role of antidepressants in treatment and challenge the idea that these medications are "happy pills." Although accounts are often mixed (cf. Karp 2007), a theme that recurs is that antidepressants do not so much alleviate sadness but allow the depressed person to reenter the world, to feel things and have them matter again, and to move in and out of these feelings without getting stuck in the fog of depression (Svenaeus 2007). Lesley Dorman describes how the antidepressant Zoloft did not deaden her feelings, nor did it make her happy. Rather, it allowed her to experience sadness and grief in an undistorted and proportional way, as the poignant, transient, and worldly feelings that they are.

> I [now] marvel at my ability to move in and out of ordinary feelings like sadness and disappointment and worry. I continue to be stunned by the purity of these feelings, by the beauty of their rightful proportion to actual life events. (2001, 241)

After taking Tofranil, a woman in her early forties describes her renewed ability to feel her way into the world in terms of "coming out of a tunnel!" (Karp 1996, 96). And poet Jane Kenyon describes how the situated meaning and significance of things returned after finding the right medication.

> We try a new drug, a new combination of drugs, and suddenly I fall into my life again. . . . I can find my way back. I know I will recognize that store where I used to buy milk and gas. . . . I remember the house and barn, the rake, the blue cups and plates, the Russian novels I loved so much. (Hall 2001, 171)

This ability to reenter and affectively engage the world reveals something about the nature of selfhood. Depression not only disrupts our relation to the world by unsettling our embodied capacities for movement and affectivity; it also weakens the uniquely human ability to *create* or *make* ourselves. Again, one of the enduring themes in Heidegger's existential phenomenology is the recognition that the human being is not to be interpreted in terms of a substance that is objectively present but in terms of the situated, self-interpreting activity of *existence*. This means there is no underlying "essence" or pregiven nature that ultimately determines who we are. We are self-creating beings structured to interpret and give meaning to our experiences. Depression can diminish this self-interpretive capacity.

THE PROBLEM OF TRANSCENDENCE

At the beginning of *Being and Time*, Heidegger explains why human beings exist in a way that is fundamentally different from other animals, a difference captured in his claim that "the 'essence' of Dasein lies in its existence" (BT, 42). The idea here is that there is no constituting essence that determines who we are. This, of course, does not mean that there are no determinate "facts" about being human. It is a fact, for instance, that I am a living organism and a person of a particular sex, that I have a unique neurochemical signature, that I live in specific geographical location and embody certain contextualized identities as a professor, for instance, or as a husband or a friend. These facts about being human, what Heidegger calls "facticity" (*Faktizität*), constitute my situation, and they limit and constrain me in certain ways (BT, 56). But Heidegger suggests that what is distinctive about Dasein is that I do not just act mechanically or instinctively on the basis of these physiological and environmental determinations. I am structured in such a way as to "transcend" or "surpass" (*übersteigen*) them by interpreting them and giving them meaning. I can, in other words, reflect on my facticity and make choices regarding how to deal with it and integrate it into my life. These choices give my life significance and direction and shape the choices I will make. We are, then, like other animals, constrained by our facticity, but we are also self-interpreting beings who in our day-to-day lives rise above or surpass our facticity by interpreting and making sense of it. This is why Heidegger insists: "Transcendence is the primordial constitution of the *subjectivity* of the subject. The subject transcends qua subject; it would not be a subject if it did not transcend" (MFL, 165).

Given this account, if I am suffering from depression, this aspect of my facticity will invariably limit and constrain me in certain ways and restrict my future possibilities. But in Heidegger's view, I am structured to care, to take a stand on my suffering by interpreting it in a particular way. I may, for instance, choose to resign myself to the situation, identify with the illness, and see it as a kind of destiny or fate. As a woman in her late twenties writes:

I've stopped thinking, "OK I'm going to get over this depression.". . . I finally
realized that well, maybe I'm in a desert. Maybe your landscape is green, but,
you know, I'm in the Sahara and I've stopped trying to get out. . . . I'd rather
cure it if I had my choice, but I don't think that is going to happen. My choice
is to integrate it into my life. So I don't see it going away. (Karp 1996, 74)

But I also have the capacity to reject the interpretation of my depression as a
maladaptive destiny and choose to embrace it as a source of wisdom and
mark of personal depth and character. A woman in her early forties, for
example, writes:

I believe that depression is actually a gift. That if we can befriend it, if we can
travel with it, that it is showing us things. Somewhere along the line we've got
to integrate it into our lives. All of us are depressed some way, somewhere, at
some time. If we don't allow it in, it can be destructive. If we allow it in, it is a
teacher. I'm saying embrace it. Be in it. (Karp 1996, 104)

In either case, in choosing to resign myself to depression or embracing it as
an opportunity for growth, Heidegger's view makes it clear that *I make
myself* who I am through my own meaning-giving choices and interpretations. Depression, then, means something to me only to the extent that it is
imbued with the value and significance that I choose to give it.

But as we saw earlier, one of the basic features of depression is the
collapse of being-in-the-world and the global deadening of affective meaning. In these cases, Heidegger's account of transcendence becomes problematic. If one of the distinguishing characteristics of being human is that we
are the only beings that are concerned about who and what we are, that our
being is an issue for us, and that we can take a stand on and give meaning to
our facticity, then would Heidegger still consider the severely depressed
person to be a self? Does he or she still embody the capacity for transcendence? Consider this woman in her early twenties who describes her depression in terms of being unable to choose or take a stand *on anything*.

My therapist, and the people in the hospital, they always said, "If you feel bad,
call somebody." [But] I'm like, "When I feel bad, I can't even get off the bed."
I'm like, "The phone is way over there." And I just look at it. I think about the
conversation that I could have with somebody, but no way am I going to pick
up the phone. [Now] I might actually take the phone with me to bed, and call
somebody from bed and say just very vaguely, "Help!" (Karp 1996, 30)

The view that Heidegger seems to be promoting suggests that even when
confronting tremendous psychic pain, the individual is invariably structured
in such a way that he or she can reflect on his or her situation, choose to
interpret it in a particular way, and take some kind of action. This is because
a person is defined on the basis of the meanings that they give to their

situation and the acts they perform in the face of it. But in cases of severe depression, the capacity for meaning-giving choices and actions is precisely the problem. As a man in his late fifties writes:

> You really can't [understand it] if you've never been to the point where it's more than you can do to get your ass out of bed and get in and take a shower. I mean, to take a shower is a major production. You can't even think, "What do I need to do [to take the shower]? How do I do this?" (Karp 1996, 42)

Indeed, depression can even problematize the idea that the individual is free to make the ultimate choice, committing suicide. This is because suicide is not passive; it is a decisive act of transcendence, one requiring a plan, ambition, and energy, and this illustrates one of the cruel ironies of depression (Alvarez 1990, 75). The individual can become so incapacitated and numb that the act of suicide itself becomes too difficult and overwhelming to imagine. "Suicide sounds terrific," writes a woman in her early thirties, "but much too difficult to plan and complete" (Karp 196, 24). Styron's description of his own vegetative depression reveals how out of reach the physical act of suicide was.

> I had reached a phase of the disorder where all sense of hope had vanished, along with the idea of futurity, my brain, in the thrall of outlaw hormones, had become less an organ of thought than an instrument of registering minute by minute, varying degrees of suffering. . . . I would lie for as long as 6 hours, stuporous and virtually paralyzed, gazing at the ceiling and waiting for that moment of evening when, mysteriously, the crucifixion would ease up just enough to allow me to force down some food and then, like an automaton, seek an hour or two of sleep again. (1990, 58)

These accounts tend to suggest that Heidegger may be overplaying Dasein's structural capacity for transcendence. This problem can be clarified if we look at the temporal aspect of depression.

Again, for Heidegger, Dasein *is time*, the horizonal movement that, out of the present, stretches backward into the past and forward into the future (BT, 185). We are, in other words, *thrown* into a factical situation that we cannot get behind, and it is against the background of this situation that we press forward (or *project*) into future possibilities. The primary temporal mode of existence in this account is futural, which means we are always "not yet" or "on the way" as we make decisions and push ahead into situated projects, careers, and relationships that will shape our identities in years to come. But this temporal coherence is often shattered in depression. When Styron, for instance, says the "the idea of futurity vanishes," he is describing how the temporal horizon contracts and closes in on him, of being trapped in the present. This is why Andrew Solomon describes depression as an atemporal experience.

> When you are depressed the past and future are absorbed entirely by the present moment, as in the world of a 3-year-old. You cannot remember a time when you felt better, at least not clearly; and you certainly cannot imagine a future time when you will feel better. Being upset, even profoundly upset, is a temporal experience, while depression is atemporal. Breakdowns leave you with no point of view. (2001, 55)

In the fog of depression, the significance and poignancy of the past no longer resonates, and the future offers no hope for recovery, for anticipated projects or possible ways of living to look forward to. All that exists is the disordered paralysis of the present moment.

Understanding existence in terms of time reveals that the world is not just the meaningful setting of our everyday lives; it is also the open space of possibilities that we are invariably pressing into. But it is a space that often closes in and collapses on the depressed person, resulting in constricted and narrowed self-interpretations. The individual finds it difficult to conceive or reframe his or her identity in any intelligible way and cannot envision other perspectives or vantage points from which to interpret himself or herself in the future. "Depression," writes a woman in her early thirties, "steals away whoever you were, prevents you from seeing who you might be someday, and replaces your life with a black hole" (Karp 1996, 24). As a result, the unique freedom we have to create ourselves and refashion our lives by moving across the country, for example, starting a family, getting married, going back to college, or changing careers becomes futile. There are no meaningful possibilities to point toward.

We see, then, that Heidegger's account of Dasein is problematic because it risks reifying the idea of the human being as a self-creating agent. When Sartre, echoing Heidegger, says that we are not born but *made* through our own meaning-giving choices, and that freedom "is the one thing that gives us dignity, the one thing that does not reduce [us] to an object" (2001, 303), he appears to overlook the extent to which depression can strip away this dignity, how it can close down our temporal horizon and capacity for forward-looking decisions. But this also reveals the value of a Heideggerian approach to psychopathology because it helps to illuminate how debilitating the depressive collapse can be. We see that in the deepest troughs of the experience, the power to make self-defining choices, a power that constitutes the very possibility of personhood, can be deadened to such an extent that the sufferer loses the capacity to exist, becoming, in Styron's words, "an automaton."

Again, the aim of these phenomenological reflections is to provide what is all too often missing in medical debates about depression, namely an account of *what it means* and *what it feels like* to be depressed by those who are actually afflicted. What is especially frustrating about the Angell affair and similar disputes in psychiatry is that the focus is almost exclusively on whether or not depression can be framed as a biochemical disease. From this initial question, a host of others are raised: "Should antidepressants be prescribed?" "Can children be properly diagnosed and should they be treated with medication?" "How should drug manufacturers market their medications?" And "How close should the relationship be between the manufacturer of drugs and the medical professionals who prescribe them?" None of these questions address the lived-experience of depression.

This is for me one of the virtues of the phenomenological approach. By letting the experience reveal itself on its own terms, the phenomenologist suspends scientific and moral judgments about what depression is or how it ought to be treated and attends instead to the self-showing of the experience. This is especially important for critics of psychiatry who claim that depression is a dubious condition and that antidepressants are useless because a biochemical cause has not been discovered. It is certainly the case that antidepressants are overprescribed and that American psychiatry is medicalizing a wider range of experiences that may simply be part of the human situation. Everyone, after all, gets sad from time to time. But when confronted with individuals who are physically incapacitated and unable to move; when they describe the world, others, and themselves as *unreal*; when the very thing that makes them human, namely, the capacity to interpret and give meaning to their own lives, is fundamentally disrupted, it seems beyond dispute that we are dealing with something that is well beyond ordinary sadness. Indeed, as we begin to understand and recognize what it means to be depressed, the rhetoric of critics like Angell begins to look ridiculous. To this end, a phenomenology of depression not only helps suffers realize that they are not alone in their experiences; it can also make families, friends, and perhaps even the staunchest critics of psychiatry more compassionate and sensitive to those who suffer as it helps to us to see the world through their eyes.

NOTES

1. To make her case, Angell pointed to a thirty-five-fold increase in mental disorders among children from 1987 to 2007 and the fact that nearly half of all Americans met the criteria for a psychiatric disorder as established by the DSM (2011a). Contributing to this epidemic, according to Angell, is the ever-increasing number of diagnostic categories in the DSM and the fact that over half of the contributors had financial ties to drug companies, "including all of contributors to the sections on mood disorders and schizophrenia"(2011b).

2. The result is that since the introduction of Prozac in 1987, "the number of people treated for depression [has] tripled . . . and about 10 percent of Americans *over the age of six* now take antidepressants" (2011a, my emphasis). Angell claims that despite its cultural pervasiveness, the chemical imbalance theory has never been empirically demonstrated. And studies have repeatedly shown that the medications used to treat these alleged imbalances are only marginal-

ly better than placebos in double-blind clinical trials. To complicate matters, drug companies tend to only publish positive results in medical journals, while the negative results usually remain unpublished. But Angell's most alarming claim is that the long-term use of antidepressants may cause a type of iatrogenic or medically induced brain damage by fundamentally altering neural functioning, making it exceedingly difficult to get off the medication (2011a).

 3. Shenk describes the difficulty of capturing the experience of depressive depersonalization in words. "Words—*unhappy, anxious, lonely*—seemed plainly inadequate, as did modifiers: *all the time, without relief.* Ordinary phrases such as *I feel bad* or *I am unhappy* seemed pallid. Evocative metaphors—*My soul is burned skin, aching at any touch. I have the emotional equivalent of a dislocated limb*—were garish. Though this language hinted at how bad I felt, it could not express what it felt like to be me" (2001, 248–49).

Chapter Three

Anxiety

Temporal Disruptions and the Collapse of Meaning

One of the initial difficulties in exploring the phenomenological aspects of anxiety is defining the term. The heterogeneity of the experience is clear in the latest incarnation of the DSM, which lists a wide range of anxiety disorders, each with its own distinct diagnostic criteria, including selective mutism, separation anxiety disorder, social anxiety disorder, agoraphobia, panic disorder, substance and medication-induced anxiety disorder, and generalized anxiety disorder (APA 2013, 189–233). Among these disorders, there is the further question of how to classify them as affective states. Is anxiety, for instance, an emotion or a mood? Again, emotions are generally regarded as being acute, episodic, and short-lived experiences that have determinate causes and are intentionally directed at specific objects or events. The fleeting and often situation-specific responses characteristic of panic disorder, agoraphobia, and social anxiety disorder appear to fit this category. Moods, on the other hand, are regarded as more indeterminate, diffused, and enduring. They are better understood as atmospheric or global affects. Like generalized anxiety disorder, mood is not a discrete episode that is caused by or directed at a specific object. It is more like a fog that negatively envelops everything. This allows us to make a distinction between people who are anxious "about" something on the one hand and those who are existentially or globally anxious on the other. In this chapter, I am primarily concerned with anxiety as a mood, and I argue that those who suffer from the emotion of anxiety in a chronic way generally experience the mood of anxiety as well. In these latter instances, anxiety captures the background sense of worry, threat, and dread that affectively shades one's experiential horizon *as a whole.*

Although the DSM is comprehensive in offering descriptions of diagnostic criteria, risk factors, differential diagnoses, and functional consequences of anxiety, it offers little to no insight into the sufferer's own experience. To this end, it fails to engage core phenomenological questions such as: "How does anxiety affect your sense of agency in the world?" "How do you make sense of, express and give meaning to your experience?" and, for the purposes of this chapter, "How does it disrupt your experience of time?" The following account focuses on how anxiety alters our physiological and cognitive timing and disturbs the embodied rhythms of everyday social life. But the primary aim, following the thread of chapter 2, is to examine how anxiety alters our self-interpretations by closing down or constricting our experience of the future. And a constricted future impedes our ability *to be* because it closes off the range of projective meanings that we would ordinarily draw on to fashion our identities.

DISTURBANCES OF EMBODIMENT AND COGNITION

Beginning with the pioneering work of psychiatrists such as Eugène Minkowski and Erwin Strauss and more recently with figures such as Thomas Fuchs, Matthew Ratcliffe, and Martin Wyllie, there has been a growing interest in drawing on the methods of phenomenology to examine how psychopathology disrupts our experience of temporality. Heidegger's work is especially helpful here because, as we have seen, temporality is already built into his account of moods, where it is only against the backdrop of our mooded situation that we can press forward or project into the future. We exist, in this view, only in the possibilities that we project for ourselves, and these possibilities mean something to us on the basis of the situation into which we have thrown. Temporality, then, is the lived-horizon of human existence that simultaneously stretches forward into the future and backward into the past, and it is the coherence and unity of this temporalizing movement or stretch that opens up a space of meaning, a "clearing" (*Lichtung*) or "there" (*Da*) that allows things to affectively matter to us.

When we are healthy and absorbed in the acts and practices of everyday life, we generally embody this temporal unity in a smooth and transparent way. This unity is revealed in the inconspicuousness of our own bodily rhythms, as respiration, heartbeat, and body temperature, as well as systems of motility and posture work in the background to structure, organize, and mediate our experience. In the seamless flow of being-in-the-world, then, I am largely unaware of my body because I am already living through it as I negotiate practical contexts, handle equipment, and engage with others. Indeed, the inconspicuousness of the body is indicative of health as the synchronized tempos of my bodily organs and motility systems do their work behind my back, maintaining their enigmatic character by remaining hidden or concealed. In episodes of mental illness, these concealed rhythms often undergo what Fuchs (2006) calls "desynchronization," indicating a disruption in this mediating activity and the conspicuous emergence of bodily functioning.

In depression, as we saw in the previous chapter, this disruption generally results in sluggishness, a slowing down or *retardation* of bodily tempos, whereas anxiety is generally experienced in terms of restlessness, speeding up, or *acceleration*. Of course, anxiety and depression are often co-occurring, which means that slowing down and speeding up can occur simultaneously in the same individual. As one woman writes:

> It's like I'm in a fog and can't fully concentrate. My words are slurred and I feel like I'm in a dream. . . . I feel extra slow like I'm moving in slow motion, but at the same time I can't hold still. My thoughts are scattered, yet I can't put them into words. . . . I get nervous to talk to co-workers because I just know my words will come out faster than my brain can put it together to make sense. (Schuster 2017)

Sufferers can experience the temporal quickening of anxiety through a number of bodily sensations, including palpitations, racing heart, sweating, trembling or shaking, and shortness of breath (APA 2013, 208). Physiological functions that were previously mediating my experience in a transparent way now surge into an explicit awareness, where I notice my body as a corporeal thing, as something *other* than me, an obtrusive and resistant object. In episodes of desynchronization, I am now aware of my heart pounding, my lungs constricting, my hands shaking, my skin flushing. In this state of temporal disruption, even the taken for granted activity of breathing can seem foreign and strange. "Your airways ignore you," writes Khaled Hosseini. "They collapse, tighten, squeeze, and suddenly you're breathing through a straw. Your mouth closes and your lips purse and all you can manage is a croak. . . . You want to scream. You would if you could. But you have to breath to scream. Panic" (2013, 128)!

In addition to the acceleration of physiological functioning, anxiety may also speed up cognitive rhythms with "racing" or "crowded" thoughts where ideas, perceptions, and memories erupt in disjointed and uncontrolled ways, making it difficult to concentrate or even causing the mind to go blank (APA 2013, 222). These rapid-fire cognitions undermine the basic temporal unity and coherence of the thought stream. In the phenomenological view, this unity is constituted by the ways in which our present awareness is structured by "protention" (intentional directedness toward the future) and "retention" (intentional directedness towards the past). The stream of consciousness is unified and bound together because, in our cognitions, "we have retentions of the preceding and protentions of the coming. . . . [And it] is through these retentions and protentions [that] the content of the stream is joined together" (Husserl 1966, 110–111). With anxiety, this self-organizing unity is broken as the mind jumps from one thought to another, resulting in speech patterns that are sped up, disorganized, and incoherent. In describing the experience, individuals refer to being "easily distracted and constantly [losing the] flow of thoughts," of having "thoughts [appear] at a rate faster than can be articulated," and feeling as if they were "watching two or three television programs simultaneously" (Piguet et al. 2009, 5). David Foster Wallace writes:

> Thoughts and associations fly through your head. . . . What goes on inside is just too fast and huge and all interconnected for words to do more than barely sketch the outlines of at most one tiny little part of it at any given instant. The internal head-speed or whatever of these ideas, memories, realizations, emotions and so on is even faster... exponentially faster, unimaginably faster. (2004, 150–51)

The acceleration and disunity of the thought stream makes it difficult to manage and control anxious thoughts. Without the structuring unity of protention and retention, thoughts take on an unrelenting life of their own. And, frustratingly, the more we try to control the thoughts, the more powerful they become. One ends up trapped in a crippling helix of worry and "what ifs." Foster Wallace captures the agony of this ruminating cycle:

> Don't think about [the thought] . . . yeah but except if I'm consciously not thinking about it then doesn't part of me have to think about it in order for me to remember what I'm not supposed to think about?. . . Shut up, quit thinking about it . . . except how can I even be talking to myself about not thinking about it unless I'm still aware of what it is I'm talking about not thinking about? (2006, 154)

The disruption of the thought stream that Foster Wallace is describing has broader implications for the psychomotor rhythms related to posture and motility, often resulting in agitation, restlessness, and impulsive behavior.

Again, my body is not an object or an assemblage of organs and parts that occupies a spatial location. And it is more than a reference to my own subjective experience. It is also a "bodily-schema," the unified sensory-motor system that anchors me to the world, constituting the phenomenal space or field that makes it possible for me to encounter and handle intraworldly things. When I am healthy, the bodily-schema seamlessly situates and coordinates my movement and position in relation to the vertical (up and down), the horizontal (front and back), and other spatial axes. In this way, it prereflectively orients me in a familiar situation or milieu. Anxiety disrupts this sensory-motor grip, pulling me out of habituated familiarity and leaving me feeling "restless, keyed up, [and] on edge" (APA 2013, 222). In this agitated state, as Raymond Carver writes, "I can hardly sit still. I keep fidgeting, crossing one leg and then the other. I could throw off sparks, or break a window—or maybe rearrange all the furniture" (1998, 375). These disruptions help to illuminate the ways in which the orienting rhythms of our embodiment do not take place in isolation; they are fundamentally relational and social, already bound up in the wider rhythms of an intercorporeal world.

My intercorporeality discloses the fact that I am not an autonomous, self-enclosed entity. I am, rather, already open and receptive to the bodies of others and can make sense of who I am only in relation to these embodied ways of being. Indeed, it is only on the basis of being engaged and involved in these shared practices and concerns that things can reveal themselves as meaningful. I understand myself through the ways in which I have been habituated and absorbed into the bodies, practices, and concerns of others. Thus, Dasein cannot be regarded as an encapsulated "subject." In fact, "the they" (*das Man*), as Heidegger reminds us, "is the 'realist subject' of everydayness" (BT, 128). Caught up in the temporal rhythms of public life, I am transparently geared and synchronized to the gestures, expressions, and movements of others. This transparency is evident in any number of shared activities, as we shuffle in unison boarding an airplane, collectively wait in line at a crowded shopping mall, share a meal in concert with others, or synch ourselves in the flow of a group conversation. Anxiety creates a sense of "time urgency" that disrupts these public rhythms, as they are generally perceived as being *too slow*. Characteristics of time urgency can be identified in speech patterns that are excessively hurried and rushed combined with feelings of frustration when someone takes too long to make a point; in walking speed that is faster than others accompanied by a sense that others are always slowing you down; in eating habits where one inhales one's food and is usually the first at the table who finishes a meal; in driving habits that involve needless annoyance when caught in slow-moving traffic and aggressive or rude gestures to speed up other drivers; and in an inability to wait that manifests in restless irritation when stuck in lines at stores and restaurants and even walking out after waiting only a short time (Levine 1997, 20–21). In *Being and Time*, Heidegger refers to this aspect of public time in terms of "curiosity" (*Neugier*), referring to a pervasive sense of "restlessness" (*Unruhe*) as a core symptom of modern life, where technologically mediated speed, busy-ness, and distractibility creates a situation of chronic sensory arousal and time pressure, where "Dasein *never [dwells] anywhere* . . . [and is] constantly uprooting itself" (BT, 172–73). Later, in *Contributions to Philosophy* (1936–1938), he refers to this in terms of "acceleration" or "speediness" (*Schnelligkeit*) embodied in a kind of "mania [where] one is unable to bear the stillness" of one's own life (CP, 83).

Although acceleration and time urgency may be out of synch with ordinary social rhythms, taken on their own, this kind of behavior does not constitute a psychopathology. But when the agitation becomes extreme, it can shatter the flow of intercorporeal time, resulting in attacks of intense anxiety in public situations. This is especially apparent in cases of agoraphobia, panic disorder, and social phobia, where using public transportation, for example, standing in line at the grocery store, or being in an enclosed space with others such as a theater or a shopping mall can trigger panic and the paralyzing feeling that "I'm trapped" or "I can't get out of here" (APA 2013, 218). When these experiences become chronic, it often results in avoidance behavior in which the sufferer actively seeks to minimize contact with public situations or events that might be triggering. Such patterns can narrow and constrict existence by closing off a range of possible undertakings and projects. One may, for example, refuse to take a promotion at work if it involves relocating or using public transportation; avoid visiting family and friends because it requires air travel; or arrange for food delivery to avoid entering crowded shops or supermarkets. In severe cases, an individual may be completely homebound or incapable of leaving the house without being accompanied by a partner or health-care professional (APA 2013, 218–19). A mother describes the experience of existential contraction in the following way:

> I avoid taking the elevator at work just to avoid possible interactions with people. I keep my head down when I pass through the office. Avoid and put off phone calls because I'm too anxious about how the person on the other line will be or what they want to discuss. I jump when phones ring, when doors slam. My daughter misses out on spending time with other kids because I'm too anxious to meet other parents. My husband misses out on many opportunities because of my anxiety; he backs out of plans or doesn't make any because he knows it will probably make me anxious to either be alone or meet new people. It impacts my family, my career, myself. (Schuster 2017)

This kind of contraction can fray social relationships and the emotional connections that nourish and sustain our self-interpretations, resulting in a downward spiral of isolating behavior and associated feelings of shame and guilt that can further exacerbate anxiety (Fuchs 2003). It can, like depression, also create a sense of affective "barrenness or emptiness" that makes it difficult to identify any worldly projects or commitments that stand out as significant or meaningful (cf. Ulmer and Schwartzburd 1996). To this end, chronic anxiety can erode away the temporal structure of existence itself, where the future is disclosed not as a horizon of accessible and worthwhile possibilities, but as a region that is fundamentally hostile and threatening. In these states, as one woman writes, "I put off everything in any way possible; I stay in bed as long as I can or spend hours pointlessly scrolling through social media because I feel anxious about doing anything for fear of being judged" (Schuster 2017). Heidegger explores the ontological consequences of this structural erosion by illuminating how it undermines one's capacity to be, that is, to understand and make sense of who one is as a person. This is why he says, "anxiety takes away from Dasein the possibility of understanding itself" (BT, 187). We can now turn to an examination of the meaning of this temporal collapse and the role it plays in disrupting the constitution of the self.

ANXIETY AS NARRATIVE FORECLOSURE

Again, unlike emotions, which are situation specific and directed at particular objects or events, moods are directed at the world *as a whole*. They are the affective atmospheres within which we dwell, disclosing the significance and meaning that our worldly projects have for us. Thus, Heidegger says moods provide the answer to the basic question: "How are you?" or "How's it going?" (*Wie befinden Sie sich?*) They reveal how the choices, relationships, and commitments we undertake matter to us in the ways that they do (BT, 137). Again, Dasein is always already thrown into a mooded situation that opens up a range of future possibilities that we can project for ourselves and through which we understand and interpret who we are. This is what Heidegger means when he says, Dasein is "ahead-of-itself-being-already-in-(the-world)" (BT, 192). We are simultaneously "ahead of itself" and "already-in," and it is the unity and coherence of this temporal structure that constitutes the horizon of meaning that allows things to reveal themselves *as such* (BP, 265). From this, it could be argued that Heidegger is forwarding a narrative conception of self, one that suggests we exist in the interpretations and stories that we create or fashion for ourselves (Guignon 1993a, 2004). The integrity of the self, in this view, is constituted by its narrative unity, by the way in which our future projects and commitments fit or cohere with the meanings of our situation. The capacity to create a story that unifies and holds together this narrative structure is essential for selfhood. But chronic anxiety can erode this capacity for narrative self-creation.

For Heidegger, what distinguishes anxiety from other kinds of moods is that it doesn't open up a range of meaningful possibilities; rather, it closes off possibilities by disclosing a world that is fundamentally meaningless. Thus, in anxiety, "the world collapses into itself; [it] has the character of completely lacking significance" (BT, 186). In this account, the world is still there; it is not absent but appears to us now as threatening and unfamiliar because its meaning and value have been drained away (Svenaeus 2011). With anxiety, nothing stands out as significant anymore; my job, my relationships, my commitments, the very things I rely on to construct a coherent and unified life-story, are stripped of their import. And this can undercut my ability to be. Heidegger, as we will see in the next chapter, refers to this as "dying"

(*Sterben*), a technical term he employs to capture the event of ontological death, of the "possibility of the *im-possiblity* of existence" (BT, 262).

The experience is analogous to what Mark Freeman (2000) calls "narrative foreclosure," in which the interpretive resources required in fashioning a coherent life-story are affectively closed off, dimming one's capacity for self-creation. Although this kind of closure occurs on a spectrum, and in *Being and Time* Heidegger appears to be describing an extreme case—that of *total* world-collapse—we can see how it might pertain to a common criterion for generalized anxiety disorder, specifically "apprehensive expectation," the pervasive worry that something bad *will happen* (APA 2013, 222). The future-directedness of this state invariably closes off possibilities that one can draw on to construct a life-story because it exposes future endeavors as threatening and bereft of any positive meaning or fulfillment. And the atmospheric quality of the mood means that it is not directed at specific objects or events; it is generalized and diffused; it is, as Heidegger says, "already 'there,' and *yet nowhere*" (BT, 186, my emphasis). Scott Stossel describes the ubiquity of the condition in this way:

> I am buffeted by worry: about my health and my family members' health; about finances; about work; about the rattle in my car and the dripping in my basement; about the encroachment of old age and inevitability of death; *about everything and nothing.* (2015, 6, my emphasis)

Narrative unity is structured by some sense of what Heidegger calls, "the for-the-sake-of-which" (*das Worumwillen*), referring to the background sense we have of our own "futurity" (*zukünftig*), that is, of who we are based on where our life-story is heading (BT, 194). But if the future is shaded by pervasive apprehension, doubt, and worry *about everything*, then there is a sense that one's story is not going anywhere; that it is already finished. Freeman refers to this phenomenon as "the death of narrative desire" (2002, 90), a death that both drains away the meaning of one's life-story as well as the desire for narrative self-creation itself by disclosing future projects and commitments as fundamentally futile. In this state, writer Donald Antrim asks:

> What do you look forward to? I look forward to poverty, abandonment by my remaining family members, the inability to write or work, the dissolution of friendships, professional and artistic oblivion, loneliness and deterioration, institutionalization and the removal from society—abjection and the end of belonging. (2019, 76)

Moreover, if existence is structured by "thrown projection," then the affective shading of anxiety does more than close off the future; it also moves backward into the past. Memories, relationships, and experiences that once stood out as pleasurable and significant are bleached out, revealing themselves as barren markers of failure, missed opportunity, and unfulfilled promise. When anxiety infects the past and future in this way, the world-disclosing power of our temporal constitution can shut down, leaving the sufferer frozen in self-doubt. "Anxiety whispers doubt into every action I take," writes one woman. "[It tells] me that nothing I do will be good enough and uses every past action as a reminder that if I was only better the result would have been better too" (Schuster 2017).

Although the DSM neglects this aspect of temporal collapse as a characteristic of anxiety disorders, Matthew Ratcliffe et al. (2014) identifies an applicable version in the symptomology of "post-traumatic stress disorder," what DSM-IV-TR refers to as a "sense of foreshortened future" (APA 2000, 468), and more broadly in DSM-V as a "persistent and exaggerated negative expectation regarding important aspects of life applied to . . . the future" (APA 2013, 275). This criterion conveys an atmospheric sense of negativity and threat, that "the world is dangerous" and that "no one can be trusted" (APA 2013, 271). When one projects this sense of danger, doubt, and lack of trust, it invariably distorts the way time is experienced; it reveals a constricted future with diminished possibilities. This is akin to the "apprehensive expectation" that characterizes chronic anxiety, where the world reveals itself as a site of breakdown and failure and, therefore, is "incompatible with the possibility of an open and progressive life story" (Ratcliffe et al. 2014, 8). This sense of foreshortened future raises unique challenges for clinicians. The temporal disturbances related to physiological functioning, cognition, and behavior discussed earlier appear to respond well to clear treatment options, usually a combination of antidepressants and short-term cognitive-behavioral therapy. But, as we have shown, when anxiety disrupts the horizon of temporality itself it disrupts the very structures or conditions that make it possible to be.

In these situations, it is not enough to address physical and behavioral symptoms. The clinician needs to engage in a dialogue that opens up new narrative possibilities for the sufferer, possibilities that help create a discursive space that allows the client to reinterpret him or herself in the face of world collapse in order to recreate or reimagine a new identity. This kind of dialogical work can illuminate worldly resources and interpretative meanings that were initially concealed or closed off, giving the person the capacity for what Heidegger calls "poetizing" (*Dichten*) or "projective saying" (*entwerfende Sagen*), a way of speaking that "brings the unsayable (*Unsagbare*) as such into the world" (OWA, 198–199). In this way, a future previously darkened by anxiety begins to gradually light up again, revealing new meanings and possibilities (Aho and Guignon 2011).

But there is a risk involved in this narrative reconfiguration that emerges out of the all-too-human longing for an identity that is fixed and secure, one that provides some sense of completion to what has been opened up in the process of self-creation. This inclination, what Paul Smith (1988) calls "claustrophilia," creates the illusion of closure, that we have regained control and mastery of our identities in the wake of world-collapse (cf. Freeman 2000). This is a familiar theme in cancer narratives where, for instance, sufferers stubbornly refuse to see themselves as victims but as warriors who never gave up, whose story is one of fighting and defeating the disease until the new identity of "survivor" can be claimed (Ehrenreich 2009, 26-27). The clinician needs to remind the sufferer that clinging to a new identity as if it were the end of the story invariably fails, not because cancer may metastasize and destroy the survivor narrative but because the structure of existence itself is vulnerable to collapse. As we will see in the next chapter, this is what Heidegger means when he says, "Dasein is dying factically . . . as long as it [exists]" (BT, 303). As anyone who has suffered from anxiety knows, the collapse of meaning does not have to have a cause or reason—cancer, job loss, divorce, etc.—rather, "*it is possible at any moment*" (BT, 302).

One of the enduring insights of Heidegger's analytic of Dasein in this regard is the recognition that our self-interpretations are always "on the way," always in the process of becoming. This means that the answer to the question "Who am I?" is ceaselessly being revised and reimagined as our choices and actions run up against the constraints and limitations of our situation. Because of this, our narrative identities can and will die any number of times throughout our lives. For Heidegger, the proper attitude is not to recoil from this experience but to be ready for it, that is, to anticipate the possibility of our own dying. He refers to this attitude in term of "resoluteness" (*Entschlossenheit*), a word that contains the literal sense of "being open" or "unlocked" (*ent* "not" + *schliessen* "to close") and is meant to capture the importance of remaining flexible and open with our own self-interpretations. Resolute Dasein, says Heidegger, "cannot become rigid as regards the situation, but must understand that resolution . . . must be held open and free for the current factical possibility" (BT, 307). Crucial to the therapeutic process, then, is helping the sufferer own up to the structural vulnerability of any narrative identity he or she happens to project for themselves, and this requires letting go of our tendency to cling to our identities as if they were somehow fixed and secure. Healing the anxious requires opening up discursive meanings and possibilities that were initially concealed by the mood. But as Heidegger reminds us, it also demands a willingness to give up on identities that are no longer livable, that is, to remain resolutely free for the possibility of "*taking it back*" (BT, 308).

We can now take a closer look at the relationship between mental illnesses, the structural instability of the self, and the experience of world-collapse by exploring Heidegger's unique account of death and dying in *Being and Time*. As we have seen, when episodes of mental illness trigger a breakdown or collapse of meaning, it undermines our ability to understand or make sense of who we are. This can be viewed as an ontological death in the sense that we cannot *be anything* because the intelligible world that we draw on to fashion our identities and sustain our sense of self has been drained of significance. As such, death poses a unique challenge to clinicians because it does not indicate the presence of a discrete medical entity that can be controlled or eradicated with chemical interventions. Rather, it belongs to the ontological constitution of Dasein itself, and it is an event that we physiologically live through, with episodes erupting numerous times throughout our lives. But, for Heidegger, this kind of death is not simply a malefic or meaningless function of the human condition. If anticipated and accepted in the appropriate way, it also contains the seeds for personal growth and transformation by illuminating the frailty and impermanence of our identities and forcing us to critically engage the choices and actions that define us.

Chapter Four

Mental Illness, Ontological Death, and Possibilities for Healing

Heidegger's account of death in *Being and Time* has been hugely influential but is often misunderstood.[1] The standard interpretation comes from Sartre in *Being and Nothingness* (1956), who suggests Heidegger's central insight regarding death rests in the distinction between the banal and self-evident awareness that "everyone will die" and the uncanny individualizing awareness that "I will die." This latter awareness discloses what Heidegger calls the "mineness" (*Jemeinigkeit*) of death, and it individualizes and overwhelms us by severing our secure and stabilizing ties to the public world, awakening us to the unsettling fact that our existence is finite and that all of our self-defining projects and commitments are ultimately futile. This existentialist interpretation leads to a particular conception of authenticity, where instead of fleeing into the tranquilizing distractions of *das Man*, the authentic individual is freed from these distractions, owns up to the finitude of existence, and lives with renewed intensity and passion, with the ever-present possibility of one's own death fully in view.[2] Here, authentic "being-towards-death" (*Sein-zum-Tode*) involves a specific orientation about one's future demise, where the possibility of one's end continually threatens, as Sartre writes, not only "at the limit of old age [but also with] sudden death which [can] annihilate us at the prime of life or in youth" (1956, 512). But the idea that Heidegger's references to being-towards-death have something to do with individualization and the fundamental precariousness of life fails to account for the nuanced distinction between three kinds of death discussed in *Being and Time*: "perishing" (*Verenden*), "demising" (*Ableben*), and "dying" (*Sterben*).[3]

The suggestion is that, for Heidegger, death does not refer to physiological "perishing" of the kind we share with other animals, nor does it necessarily refer to the individualizing dread of one's own physical "demise" that the authentic individual must face in order to live more freely. Indeed, if we recall how Heidegger defines human existence in terms of being-in-the-world, a peculiar picture of death begins to emerge. It is not necessarily a terminal event that happens at the end of one's life. It is, rather, a kind of collapse or "breakdown" (*Zusammenbruch*) of meaning itself, where what dies or comes to an end is not physiological functioning but the ability to understand and make sense of the world and oneself. From the perspective of mental illness, then, death refers to the uncanny experience of having one's way of being or identity slip away because the familiar world dissolves into meaninglessness. This is ontological death in the sense that I cannot *be anything* because the relational background of equipment, roles, relationships, and practices that I draw on to fashion my identity and sustain my sense of self has lost all significance for me. I am, quite simply "*unable-to-be.*" Accordingly, what Heidegger calls "dying" (*Sterben*) is not only an event that I can physiologically *live through*; it is an event that discloses the structural vulnerability at the core of my existence and, as often happens with episodes of mental illness, can occur a number of times throughout my life.

In this chapter, we explore what Heidegger means by dying and attempt to concretize the experience by drawing on first-person narratives of critical illness. These narratives provide a vivid point of entry into the experience of world-collapse and bring to the surface both the affective loss of identity and the therapeutic challenge of reintegrating oneself back into a context of meaning in the wake of this loss. A narrative is not simply a subjective report that can be used as technical datum that corresponds to various categories of disorder in the DSM. It is, rather, the opening up of a discursive framework that allows the individual to make sense of and give meaning to his or her experience and identity as a whole. Narrative, in this sense, both *expresses* the lived-reality of the experience, but it also *constitutes* the significance of that reality (Taylor 1985; Schultz & Flasher 2011). As we saw in the previous chapter, it can be argued that Heidegger forwards a narrative conception of self in which our identities are held together and constituted by the stories we create about ourselves, and these stories have the power to express *what it means* to experience world-collapse. But they also provide an opportunity to construct alternative interpretations amidst the debris and anguish of self-loss, and in this respect represent an important opportunity for healing. In the dialogical to and fro between psychiatrist and patient, a new story can be fashioned, one that acknowledges and is open to the fundamental vulnerability of our identities and flexible enough to let go of those that have lost their significance or viability.

WHY DASEIN DOES NOT PERISH

In §49 of *Being and Time*, Heidegger introduces his distinction between perishing, demising, and dying. He refers to perishing as the kind of death that is "appropriate to anything that lives," yet goes on to say, "Dasein never perishes" (BT, 247). But if Dasein is a reference to human existence, and existence has something to do with *being alive*, then what are to make of this apparent contradiction? The answer, of course, rests in the unique way that Heidegger defines Dasein, making it clear it should be regarded not as a living organism or biochemical substance but as a situated, self-interpreting *way of being*. Again, Dasein's existence is constituted not by "*what* it is" but by "*how* it is," that is, by how it understands and interprets itself within and against a context of shared meanings. It is our particular way of understanding and making sense of things that constitutes our "*ability-to-be*."

To say that Dasein is "alive," then, has little to do with physiological processes. The fact that the human being has a heart that pumps blood or neural circuits that transmit signals to various parts of the body is not Heidegger's primary concern. His focus is the "question of being" (*Seinsfrage*), a question that attempts "to lay bare the horizon within which something like being in general becomes intelligible [and] . . . clarifying the possibility of having any understanding of being at all—an understanding that belongs to the constitution of the entity called Dasein" (BT, 231). It is therefore the existential conditions or structures that make it possible for us to interpret and give meaning to the physiological processes of the body that is important, not the deterministic process itself. And it is this interpretative activity—our understanding of being—that distinguishes Dasein from other animals. Dasein lives or exists only as being-in-the-world, hence Heidegger's controversial claim that the existence of animals is always impoverished or "world-poor" (*weltarm*) because they are deprived of the ability to interpret and give meaning to things on the basis of involvement in a shared historical context. Heidegger makes this point explicit when he articulates the difference between the reductive and deterministic conception of life formulated in the natural sciences from the "factical life" (*faktische Leben*) of humans. For Heidegger, human life is already bound up in a world, and this enmeshment shapes the possible ways in which I care *for* and *about* things, those self-defining roles, projects, and commitments that are important and matter to me in fashioning my identity. This means Dasein is alive only to the extent that it is absorbed in and understands the world, an understanding enables Dasein to be who it is. The animal, by contrast, is trapped in the "ring" (*Umring*) of its own instincts; it is deprived of the ability to create and sustain a meaningful identity, and, for this reason, it "behaves within an environment but never within a world" (FCM, 239). Determined in this way, the animal does not have a historical identity to lose. Heidegger explains:

Thus, just as it remains questionable to speak of an organism as a historical (*geschichtlich*) or even historiological being, it is questionable whether death for man and death for an animal are the same, even though physiochemical, physiological correlations can be ascertained. (FCM, 267)

It is on the basis of this difference that Heidegger can say: "Only man dies, the animal [merely] perishes" (TT, 176).

Now we have a clearer sense of what Heidegger means when he says, "Dasein never perishes." It is the physiological body that comes to an end when we perish, not our understanding of being. Of course, this is not to say our understanding of being is akin to some immaterial substance or soul that continues to exist after life-sustaining biological processes cease. Again, Dasein is not to be confused with a substance. It is a self-interpreting activity, and it is this activity that dies in ontological death. What is especially unsettling, in the context of mental illness, is that such a death occurs while the physical body is still very much alive. Again, Heidegger clarifies this distinction by making it clear that Dasein does not refer to a "corporeal thing" (*Körperding*) (BT, 238), and this helps explain why there are so few references to the body in *Being and Time*. One of the central aims of his early project was to dismantle the naturalistic assumption that the human being is to be regarded as a kind of physical substance that has extension, material composition, and causal determinations. For Heidegger, such a view fails to account for *my own* body that is always already involved in the world. The body, in this view, is not a biophysical machine; it is *how* we live and experience things on the basis of our own understanding of being. Of course, Heidegger is not denying that our understanding of being is "in each case dispersed in a body" (MFL, 137), but a scientific account of the natural body has little to do with our existence or *way of being*, that is, how we interpret, experience, and give meaning to the world and ourselves.

Here, the limitations of a biological view of death are clearly exposed. When Heidegger refers to the "medical concept of '*exitus*'" (BT, 241), he is showing that it does not refer to the death of Dasein. He is, rather, pointing to the structural vulnerability of both the world as a disclosive site of meaning and of our own self-interpretations. Although he does not offer a developmental account of Dasein, the implication is that at the point I begin to make sense of the world and interpret my identity as something that matters to me—as a good son, for example, or a loyal friend—that particular identity is capable of coming to an end. But when *every* meaningful identity or self-interpretation breaks down, as in cases of severe mental illness, one undergoes an ontological death. This is a kind of death that is not possible for a newborn infant or child that is not alive in the sense of being-in-the-world. "Dying" is a possibility only for Dasein. It is, as Heidegger says, "*a way to be*, which Dasein takes over as soon as it is" (BT, 245, my emphasis). *Not yet*

Dasein in infancy can, of course, occur at the other end of the life cycle as well, when one may *no longer* be Dasein in the confusion and dementia of old age. Although he briefly alludes to this when he says, "Dasein may well have passed its ripeness before the end" (BT, 244), one of the stronger criticisms leveled against *Being and Time* is that we are introduced only to a strong and healthy incarnation of Dasein, one that is seamlessly engaged in meaningful, goal-directed projects and skillfully handling the tools of the workshop, as if this is the only manifestation of human existence we encounter in everydayness. There are, as John Caputo remarks, "no beggars, lepers, hospitals, homeless people, [or] children" in Heidegger's world (1994, 332). Caputo's comments are especially relevant to our topic because, as we will see, the experience of illness can illuminate the phenomenon of ontological death and helps provide a more nuanced and expansive view of the experience.

THE DEMISE OF DASEIN

The difference between perishing and demising, for Heidegger, can be understood in terms of the relationship between the two views of the body introduced earlier. Perishing is the death of *Körper*, whereas demising relates to *Leib*, to how we affectively experience, interpret, and give meaning to our impending physical death. And because demise involves the capacity to be aware of, to understand, and even shudder in the face of death, it is exclusive to Dasein. The existentialist interpretation generally suggests that because our physical existence is contingent and finite, all of our self-defining projects are in the end futile and meaningless. The mood of atmospheric dread that accompanies this awareness is the existentialist version of death-anxiety. Tolstoy offers a classic account of this experience in his memoirs:

> I could not attribute a reasonable motive to any single act in my whole life. I was only astonished that I could not have realized this at the very beginning. All of this had so long ago been known to me! Illness and death would come . . . to those whom I loved, to myself, and nothing remains but stench and worms. All my acts, whatever I did, would sooner or later be forgotten, and I myself [would] be nowhere. Why, then, busy oneself with anything? (1994, 16)

Perishing and demising, then, are not different in degree but different in kind. When Heidegger claims, "The essence of Dasein lies in its existence" (BT, 42), he is making it clear the human being is not a biophysical thing with a fixed, predetermined nature. We exist *for ourselves* as self-making beings that are always capable of interpreting our physiological givenness. As a self-making activity, there is nothing that fundamentally grounds or secures my existence; I am a "not yet" or a "being possible," always in the process of constituting and making myself who I am until my existence comes to an end. But Heidegger goes on to argue that the activity of self-making is not only vulnerable to collapse when I am affectively confronted with the end of my life. It is vulnerable *at any time*; it is subject to a *"constant threat arising from Dasein* [itself]" (BT, 265). This means my ability-to-be, even when relatively young and healthy, is something that cannot be taken for granted, and the anxiety arising from ontological death cannot be deferred by the idea that it will happen only in the distant future when my body weakens and begins to fail me in sickness and old age. This explains why Heidegger says, "medical and biological investigations . . . can obtain results which may become significant ontologically [only] if the basic orientation for an existential interpretation of death has been made secure" (BT, 247). As existentialists have argued, my impending biological death gains its meaning from the fact that I am an ontological being, that I can take a stand on and interpret my own death by investing it with the significance that it has. The horror that flashes in the lucid awareness of death is a world-collapse insofar as it exposes the radical contingency and finitude of my projects and forces me to confront the ultimate questions: "Who am I?" and "How should I live?" But the fact that the terminal event can be pushed away into some vague and distant future makes it easier to deny, turning the uncanny anxiety of our own structural "nothing-ness" into a much more manageable fear "of something."

The distinction between fear and anxiety is central to understanding the distinction between demising and dying (cf. Thomson 2013). For Heidegger, "fear" (*Furcht*) has the characteristic of an emotion insofar as it has a determinate cause and is intentionally directed at specific objects or events; it "always comes from entities [things or events] within-the-world," whereas "anxiety" (*Angst*) comes from *"nothing and nowhere"* (BT, 187). Thus, the experience of world-collapse that emerges in the awareness of my impending physical death can be interpreted as fear. And because this fear is of something, a future event, it can be located and managed to some extent as something external, as not yet belonging to me. Heidegger suggests this view actually "weakens [death] by calculating how we are to have it at our disposal" (BT, 261). Contrast this with the diffuse mood of anxiety, where there is nothing I can point to or indicate what it is that I am anxious about. This is because the vulnerability of world-collapse belongs not to my future end but to the ontological structure of my existence itself and, as such, *"it is possible at any moment"* (BT, 258).[4] When our structural vulnerability erupts in anxiety, it destroys our familiar way of making sense of things. We die because "the 'world' can offer nothing more, [and this] takes away from Dasein the possibility of understanding itself" (BT, 187). We see then that when Heidegger refers to dying, he is agreeing with the existentialist account, but he is also making a stronger claim. The collapse of our self-understanding does not just occur in the painful awareness of our impending physical death because our identity is already unstable, already structured by the possibility of its own collapse. This is why Heidegger says, "Dasein is dying factically and indeed constantly, as long as it has not yet come to its demise" (BT, 259), and later, "Dasein does not have an end at which it simply stops, [rather] it *exists finitely*" (BT, 329). I want to suggest that to "exist finitely" is to be in such a way that is always vulnerable to world-collapse, which effectively puts an end to our ability-to-be. As opposed to demising, then, dying is the "possibility of the *im-possibility* of existence . . . [and] is not 'added on' to Dasein at its 'end'" (BT, 306). This account helps to illuminate what is especially frightening about episodes of mental illness, where we experience and suffer through the collapse of our world and the paralyzing dissolution of the self. We are simultaneously alive and dead; we continue to perceive, handle, and experience things, but we are unable to attribute meaning or significance to any of it.

In these moments, activities and projects that used to be pleasurable lose all significance, future events are stripped of their affective resonance, and the motivation to move forward and engage with the world breaks down. But for Heidegger, these episodes do not indicate the presence of a medical condition that can be controlled or eradicated by balancing neurochemistry with medication. Anxiety cannot be fixed by medical interventions because it belongs to the ontological constitution of Dasein itself. On this account, biomedical explanations fail to grasp the significance of ontological death because they are unable to "interpret [anxiety] according to the principles of its existential-ontological constitution" (BT, 190). Thus, Heidegger says, "Only because Dasein is anxious in the very depths of its being, does it become possible for anxiety to be elicited physiologically" (BT, 190). This does not necessarily mean, however, that everyone suffers from death-anxiety but, rather, that it is always a possibility due to the structural vulnerability of our own self-interpretations.[5] At the same time, dying is not simply a meaningless and inimical shattering of the self. For Heidegger, if we anticipate it in a particular way, it also presents an opportunity for personal growth and transformation by exposing the frailty and impermanence of our identities, forcing us to confront the choices and actions that make us who we are and opening us up to the possibility of alternative self-interpretations.

When in the face of ontological death we cling to our publicly interpreted identities or flee back into its comforts after the moment has passed, we are "inauthentic" (*uneigentlich*), unwilling to own up to our structural vulnerability. This kind of denial or evasion is, for Heidegger, our usual response to dying. It is how Dasein "maintains itself proximally and for the most part" (BT, 260). As we saw in the previous chapter, in order to be authentic, Heidegger refers to the importance of "resoluteness" (*Entschlossenheit*), understood as a kind of unwavering readiness to die, to anticipate the pos-

Chapter 4

sibility of world-collapse. In anticipatory resoluteness, "[Dasein] takes over authentically in its existence the fact that it *is* the null basis of its own nullity" (BT, 306). The use of the word "resoluteness" is a bit misleading because it could easily be read as a kind of unyielding single-mindedness, the same attitude inauthentic Dasein embodies in denying death by stubbornly clinging to a familiar identity. But for Heidegger, *Entschlossenheit* signifies an attitude of receptivity and openness to the contingency of my existence and a steady, clear-eyed willingness to be flexible with how I interpret myself and to let go of those self-interpretations that are no longer viable. Thus, whatever identity I happen to choose or commit myself to at a given time, I have to always "hold [myself] free for the possibility of *taking it back*" (BT, 308). When we respond to death-anxiety in this way, we are able to let go or give up on the notion that there is something stable and enduring about who we are, making it possible for us to own up to our structural vulnerability and be released from inauthentic clinging. Anticipating and being ready for death in this way "discloses to existence that its uttermost possibility lies in *giving itself up*, and thus it shatters all one's tenaciousness to whatever existence one has reached" (BT, 308, my emphasis).

Interestingly, Heidegger appears to suggest that the transformative and emancipatory possibilities of authenticity may be out of reach for most people. This is attributed to what he calls the "ascendency of falling and publicness" (BT, 190), a pervasive social conformism or "leveling down" (*Einebnen*) entrenched in our everyday social practices and cultural institutions, creating the illusion there is something timeless, substantial, and enduring about our being. This, in turn, covers over an awareness of our own finitude, which apparently for Heidegger makes the experience of "genuine" or "real anxiety" (*eigentliche Angst)* exceedingly rare (BT, 190).[6] From this, a romantic picture of authenticity begins to emerge as something like a privilege, exclusive to those sensitive enough to experience the affective power of anxiety and to see through the distortive and corrosive influence of *das Man*.[7] This is why approaching the phenomenon of ontological death from the perspective of critical illness—rather than from what Heidegger calls "the factical rarity of anxiety" (*die faktische Seltenheit des Angstphänomens*) (BT, 190)—can be especially useful. *Das Man*, after all, cannot shield us from the frailty of our own bodies. Aging and illness are not factically rare; they are inescapable in the course of living a life, and they point both to our terminal end in demise and our structural vulnerability in dying. And, as a reminder of the precariousness of our self-constitution, they illuminate the importance of being willing to give up on one's identity in the wake of world-collapse.

ONTOLOGICAL DEATH AND ILLNESS NARRATIVES

Heidegger never explores how ontological death may be triggered by the trauma of critical illness. But if we look at recurrent themes in illness narratives, we see that they capture many of the affective aspects of ontological death. These accounts help to expand the narrow neurochemical view of suffering to address the existential and ontological pain that invariably accompanies world-collapse. Medical sociologist Kathy Charmaz describes this latter kind of suffering in terms of a "crumbling away of their former self-image without simultaneous development of equally valued new ones. The experiences and meanings upon which these ill persons had built former positive self-images are no longer available to them" (1983, 168).[8] Here, Heidegger's account of authentic being-towards-death is particular instructive, as it not only cultivates a clear-sighted acceptance of the structural vulnerability of our self-interpretations but also fosters a willingness to let go of identities that no longer resonate or fit in the world of the critically ill. This flexibility makes it possible to be more open and responsive to alternative meanings in order to narrate a new self-interpretation. Arthur Frank's memoir *At the Will of the Body* (1991) offers a rich and compelling example of these overlapping themes.

After having a heart attack at the age of thirty-nine and then being diagnosed with testicular cancer at forty, Frank describes the affective horror that erupts with the collapse of meanings that held his former identity together. "Your relationships," he writes, "your work, your sense of *who you are* and *who you might become*, your sense of what life is and ought to be—these all change, and the change is terrifying" (1991, 6, my emphasis). This collapse is amplified when Frank enters the technological world of medical expertise and experiences the self-estrangement that comes from being reduced to a corporeal object with little recognition by the doctors of what it means to experience critical illness.

Illuminating the distinction between *Körper* and *Leib*, he writes, "What happens when my body breaks down happens not just to that body but also to my life, which is lived in that body. When the body breaks down, so does the life" (1991, 10). He found that in the clinical encounter, "*my* body, my ongoing experience of being alive, becomes *the* body, an object to be measured and objectified" (1991, 12). The reluctance or inability of Frank's doctors to acknowledge his lived-experience not only points to the limits of the biomedical interpretation of suffering. It also reveals how the detached and objectifying language of scientific medicine—one that refers to disease as an "it" that can be quantified and controlled—helps to shield us from our own structural vulnerability. But taking this view is a mistake for the sufferer because the "ill person is forgetting that she exists as part of 'it'" (1991, 13). The sufferer is invariably forced to ask: "What's happening to *me*? Not *it*, but *me*" (1991, 13). In this way, critical illness has the power to bring to light the core aspect of our ontological constitution, an aspect that, when healthy, remains largely concealed.

With a narrative that expresses and gives meaning to his experience, Frank describes the confrontation with what Heidegger calls "the null basis of [his] own nullity." Experiencing the frailty of his body discloses the more fundamental frailty of his own being. When healthy, Frank's world held open a future, an expansive horizon of meanings and possibilities that he could draw on to create himself and hold his identity together. With the world-collapse that accompanied his illness, "the future disappeared" (1991, 127). Much of the horror he experienced involved having to live through the death of his identity. The world was still there, but it no longer made sense to him; it was uncanny or "un-homelike" (Svenaeus 2011), showing up in ways that felt unfamiliar and strange. Frank describes it in terms of "walking through a nightmare that was unreal but utterly real" (1991, 27). He quickly found that the objectifying discourse of biomedical science devalued his experience of unreality and realized that those who best recognized and affirmed what he was going through were not health-care professionals but those who had undergone the experience of critical illness themselves.[9] It was through their recognition, in "looking at [him] clearly and accept[ing] what they saw" (1991, 104) that they, in many ways, became his primary caregivers, attending to him *as a person* as opposed to the objective metrics of a disease. The doctors and nurses, of course, helped his physical body recover, but his fellow sufferers provided the recognition and the discursive context he needed to meaningfully express and make sense of his shattered identity.

With this community, Frank was able to work through his own ontological death, to give it significance, and, drawing on his relationship with fellow sufferers, create a new identity in its aftermath. Through this narrative refashioning, he was able to see the value of his suffering. It not only gave him "permission to slow down" in the face of careerism and workday busy-ness. More importantly, it allowed him to see how he was living before the illness, and this provided a sense of proportion, a sense of what really mattered in life "that is [often] lost when we take [our health] for granted" (1991, 120). When he was healthy, Frank was caught up in the harried commitments of his professional identity and was largely unaware of why he was living the way he did. Blindly "fulfilling the demands of some system" (1991, 119), Frank spent his time busily adding lines to his curriculum vitae, as if publishing another article or chairing another committee would somehow make him more substantial and real. Illness shattered this façade, forcing him to confront and ultimately let go of his self-interpretation as an ambitious and productive scholar. Letting go in this way opened him up to the poignant impermanence of being human and to the fragile web of relationships that held his identity together. "The ultimate value of illness," he writes, "is that it teaches us the value of being alive; this is why the ill are not just charity cases, but a presence to be valued. Illness, and ultimately, death remind us of living. . . . Death is no enemy of life; it restores our sense of the value of living" (1991, 120). But we now see that when Frank is referring to "death," he is not simply referring to a biological terminus but to the structural vulnerability of his identity, a vulnerability that pierced the shell of his public persona and brought to the surface meanings and values that had long been hidden.

Frank's account of personal transformation helps to concretize Heidegger's conception of authenticity. Authenticity for Heidegger has little to do with recovering some "real" or "genuine" (*eigentliche*) self that lies below the superficial crust of everydayness. Rather, it opens us up to the realization that the very idea of a real or genuine self is nothing more than an illusion, "a dubious fabrication of the public world" (BT, 278).[10] Convinced that there is something fundamentally reliable and dependable about our self-interpretations, we remain "lost in *das Man*" (BT, 383), oblivious to our structural frailty. The anxiety that erupted in the wake of Frank's illness destroyed this illusion, exposing the fact that his identity is constituted by a *lack*. In making sense of this lack and resolutely anticipating his own death, Frank constructs a new identity, one that is more free and open to a wider range of self-creating projects, not just the narrow and leveled-down fads of *das Man*, where a life based on productivity, busy-ness, and the piling up of accomplishments and material possessions is viewed as *the only way* to live.[11] But authentic resoluteness also requires a sober recognition that none of these projects results in an identity that is in any way enduring and fixed, and this why it demands the courage and "steadiness" (*Beständigkeit*) to be flexible, to be willing to give up on an identity when the situation changes (BT, 322). Understood this way, resoluteness not only helps prepare us for the inevitable movement toward old age, disease, and death; it can also prepare us for the many "little deaths" of world collapse when we get divorced or lose a job; when a child goes off to college or a parent dies. Facing these deaths with anticipatory resoluteness has the power to open us up, releasing us from the comfortable illusion that there is something stable and constant about who we are. It manifests what Heidegger calls "an impassioned *freedom-towards-death*—a freedom which has been released from the illusions of '*das Man*'" (BT, 266). This freedom is embodied in the ways authentic Dasein remains flexible with regard to his or her identity, fashioning and refashioning self-interpretations to fit the emergencies and upheavals of life.

Reading Heidegger's account of death through the lens of illness narratives helps us to better understand what he means when he says, "Dasein is dying as long as it exists" (BT, 251). Illness reminds us not only of the frailty and vulnerability of our physical bodies but of the structural vulnerability of our own self-understanding and ability-to-be. And this insight allows us to rethink the responsibilities of care. Care for the critically ill cannot be reduced to treating and measuring the diseased body. As recent advances in palliative and end-of-life care have shown, it also involves an empathic attentiveness to the individual's struggle to understand and make sense of the experience of world-collapse. As Frank's narrative makes clear, this requires the clinician to first acknowledge the existential anxiety and confusion that accompanies the loss of self. It also calls for the clinician to open up a discursive context for the sufferer to express and give meaning to his or her experience in a way that is both accepting of the structural vulnerability of each person's self-interpretation and flexible enough to give up on those that no longer resonate to their radically altered world. And finally, the clinician is challenged to offer up alternative frameworks of meaning to help the sufferer refashion or poetize a new story and a new identity in the wake of what is given in illness. As existential psychotherapist Hans Cohn writes:

> Therapy . . . could enable us to accept the inevitable characteristics of existence—like our being in the body, being with others, the necessity of choice, the certainty of death. But it could also help us to affirm the possibility of choosing our own specific responses to what is "given." (1997, 125)

Of course, rethinking care in this way extends well beyond the domain of the critically ill. We don't need to endure a heart attack or cancer to undergo an ontological death. As Heidegger says, our self-understanding can collapse in "the most innocuous situations" (BT, 189). The question is: How do we respond to this collapse? Do we recoil from it and stubbornly cling to what is familiar? Or, do we accept it and open ourselves up to the contingency and vulnerability of the world and of ourselves?

NOTES

1. There has been a great deal of discussion on the meaning of death in Heidegger's thought in recent years. Some of the more influential Anglophone interpretations can be found in Blattner (1994, 2009), Carman (2003), Guignon (1984, 2011), Haugland (2000), Hoffman (1993), Mulhall (2005), Thomson (2013), and White (2005). For a concise overview of leading interpretations of Heidegger on death, see Dreyfus (1990).

2. This interpretation is supported by the fact the Heidegger's discussion of the myriad ways in which we cover over and evade the "mineness" of death is deeply influenced by Tolstoy's *The Death of Ivan Ilych*, a story that provides what is arguably the definitive existentialist account of death (BT, 254n12).

3. In articulating this distinction, I am especially indebted to the work of William Blattner (1994) and Iain Thomson (2013).

4. Interpreting world-collapse as a structure of Dasein helps explain what Heidegger means when he says, "The 'nothing' exhibits itself as that in the face of which one has anxiety, this means that *being-in-the world* [or Dasein] *itself is that in the face of which anxiety is anxious*" (BT, 187).

5. This is why Heidegger can say that ontological death is both "certain" (*gewiss*) and "indefinite" (*unbestimmt*). *Das Man* "covers up what is peculiar in death's certainty—that it is

possible at any moment. Along with the certainty of death goes the indefiniteness of its 'when'" (BT, 258). Death is certain in the sense that the self-interpretive activity of being human is structured in a way that is always vulnerable to collapse, but it is indefinite in the sense that we have no idea if and when this collapse will happen.

6. Heidegger explains, "the rarity of the phenomenon [of anxiety] is an index that Dasein . . . remains concealed from itself . . . because of the way in which things have been publicly interpreted by 'the Anyone'" (BT, 190).

7. Heidegger also mentions that, "anxiety is often conditioned by 'physiological factors'" (BT, 190). It is unclear what this means, but it may suggest that the strength or weakness of one's nervous system conditions the force or affective experience of death-anxiety.

8. The data in Charmaz's study comes from "73 in-depth interviews with 57 chronically ill persons in northern California who have various diagnoses such as cardiovascular disease, diabetes, cancer, multiple sclerosis, lupus erythematosus and so forth" (1983, 171).

9. Frank writes, for instance, of the ways in which his nurses focused only on his physical suffering, how they refused to use the word "cancer" around him, referring to him as the "seminoma in [room] 53," and how they frequently cited other patients as being "much worse off" than he was (1991, 100–101). Indeed, the only way he could get his surgeon to slow down and have a meaningful conversation with him about his experience of suffering was by refusing to sign the consent form.

10. This, of course, does not mean that Heidegger is promoting a kind of postmodern dismissal of selfhood. The interpretive activity of Dasein provides a relatively cohesive and unified sense of self as a whole. The problem arises when I confuse the interpretive cohesiveness of my identity with permanence and become convinced that the interpretation I have of myself is the "real me."

11. It is important to note that Heidegger rejects the existentialist (e.g., Sartre's) conception of the radical or absolute subject who creates his or her identity *ex nihilo*. This is because the meaning and significance of any identity Dasein commits to in the wake of ontological death has already been established and interpreted by the public world. In short, Dasein, whether authentic or inauthentic, is never "world-less." This is why Heidegger says, "Resoluteness, as *authentic being-one's-self*, does not detach Dasein from its world, nor does it isolate it so that it becomes a free-floating 'I.' And how should it, when resoluteness as authentic disclosedness, is *authentically* nothing else than being-in-the-world? Resoluteness brings the self right into its current concernful being-alongside that is ready-to-hand, and pushes it into solicitous being with others" (BT, 298).

Part Two

Hermeneutic Psychiatry

Chapter Five

Situating Mental Illness

On the Value of Hermeneutic Psychiatry

In 1986, Heidegger's former student Hans-Georg Gadamer published a short essay entitled "Bodily Experience and the Limits of Objectification," which described the ways in which modern medical science has resulted in what he calls a "massive alienation" (*gewaltige Verfremdung*) from ourselves as situated and embodied beings (1996, 70). The aim of this chapter is to articulate the inseparability of the "lived-body" (*Leib*) from "life" (*Leben*) and explore how modern medicine, rooted as it is in the methodology of natural science, operates under an objectifying framework that is fundamentally incapable of seeing this connection. By bringing "hermeneutic awareness" (*hermeneutisches Bewußtsein*) to the phenomenon of embodiment, Gadamer not only attempts to identity the boundaries or limits of objectification in medicine but also offers a rich framework for experiential analysis of mental illness. This kind of hermeneutic awareness problematizes the assumptions of diagnostic precision and methodological neutrality espoused by biopsychiatry and the architects of the DSM. It reveals that such a standpoint is not value neutral at all because it is already embedded in the core prejudices of natural science that emerged in the Enlightenment, interpreting mental disorders from the same objectifying and mechanistic standpoint that modern medicine inherits from Cartesian and empiricist epistemologies.[1] This standpoint is constituted by "prejudgments" about what is valuable. For instance, it downplays our situated being-in-the-world by privileging a disposition of theoretical detachment and objectivity. It emphasizes the instrumental control and demonstration of knowledge characterized by a technical procedure or method. And it adopts a mechanistic picture of self and world as an aggregate of physical objects in causal interaction.

The result is a very narrow interpretation of the self as a decontextualized, causally determined object, where the sufferer is reduced to a collection of symptoms that are explained in terms of chemical imbalances in the brain. Hermeneutic psychologist Philip Cushman describes how the architects of the DSM have taken this standpoint to reconfigure the self as a set of discrete data points.

> The shift [in the DSM] implies a self no longer characterized by complex interactive patterns of holistic personality styles but made up of data points of public, observable, behavioral acts that are declared symptoms and signs by the DSM experts. The DSM self is a kind of tinker-toy self, composed of concrete, singular behaviors that can be easily disconnected and reconnected to one another in order to form the larger—but momentary—self configurations. There is little that is complex, indeterminate, and ambiguous. (Cushman 2003, 108)

Although this mechanistic view may be largely uncontroversial in the natural sciences, its application to human existence is far from persuasive, primarily because the model overlooks what it means to be human in the first place. This is why it is important for psychiatry to incorporate a hermeneutic orientation into clinical practice, one that offers an interpretation of the sufferer's own concrete and situated way of being-in-the-world. Here, of course, "world" (*Welt*) is not understood mechanistically as an aggregate of *real* physical objects in causal interaction; it is, rather, the horizon of historical meanings into which we are already thrown. Heidegger's use of the word "history" (*Geschichte*) in this context is not to be confused with a "science of history" or "historical enquiry" (*Historie*); it is, rather, the epochal movement or "happening" (*Geschehen*) through which meaning is disclosed or given to Dasein. The underlying aim of a hermeneutic approach to psychopathology, then, is to "lay bare" or "uncover" (*freilegen*) the disclosive horizon that allows mental illness to affectively manifest or reveal itself as such.

To this end, hermeneutic psychiatry exposes the uncritical assumptions inherent in the medical model and its reliance on the principles of methodological detachment, objectivity, and neutrality. When prominent psychiatrists such as Richard Wyatt, for example, claim that the DSM "attempt[s] to describe things *as they are* . . . [with a] movement towards clear, unambiguous description of psychiatric syndromes" (cited in Lewis, 2006, 5, my emphasis), the hermeneutic approach counters that there is no way to unambiguously describe disorders *as they are* because any description is already preshaped by the values and meanings opened up to us as "historical" (*geschichtlich*) beings. Situating mental illness in this way helps explain, for instance, how specific socio-historical conditions and political upheavals in the 1960s and 1970s radically changed the content of the DSM, resulting in the declassification of homosexuality as a mental disorder and the recognition of post-traumatic stress disorder for Vietnam veterans (Kutchins and Kirk 1997). What this reveals is that psychiatry does not discover transhistorical truths about the human condition; rather, as the prejudices of the world change, so do the truths of psychiatry. What is required of clinicians, then, is a fundamental "recognition that all understanding involves some prejudice" (Gadamer 1994, 270). By recognizing the extent to which it is shaped by the prejudices of its own context, psychiatry can also begin to see how suffering is situated and made intelligible. This point can be clarified by drawing a distinction between epistemological and ontological hermeneutics (cf. Ricoeur 1981).

EPISTEMOLOGICAL AND ONTOLOGICAL HERMENEUTICS

The epistemological approach to hermeneutics takes its definitive form in the work of Wilhelm Dilthey, who attempted to offer a methodological account of the "human sciences" (*Geisteswissenschaften*) that broke with the representational models of knowledge that characterize the "natural sciences" (*Naturwissenschaften*). The epistemological view of the natural sciences takes its cue largely from early modern figures like Newton, Galileo, and Descartes. These philosophers establish the idea of "certainty" as the foundation for any genuine knowledge and that the criteria for certainty hinges on experiential or ocular verification that can then be abstracted into mathematical laws. Gadamer explains:

> In the seventeenth century, experience ceased to be a source or starting point of knowledge but became, in the sense of "experiment," a tribunal of verification before which the validity of mathematically projected laws could be confirmed or refuted. Galileo did not happen to acquire the laws of free-falling objects from experience . . . they came from conceptual projection: "*mente concipio,*" that is, "I conceive"—or more precisely, "I project in my mind." What Galileo thus "projected" in his idea of a free-falling object was certainly no object of experience: a vacuum does not exist in nature. What he understood, however, precisely by this abstraction were laws within the skein of causal relationships, which are intertwined and cannot be disentangled in concrete experience. (1996, 5)

Here we have the groundwork of the *Naturwissenschaften* laid out. First, we get a dualistic view of the world, where material objects are separate and distinct from the cognizing subject, and these objects have spatial extension and are in causal interaction with other objects. Second, this view assumes the ability of the scientist to abstract or pull objects out of their relational context. This means encountering objects from the anonymous and desituated perspective of theoretical detachment, as valueless matter in a spatiotemporal coordinate system. Finally, we see the methodological aim as one that attempts to explain the causal interactions of objects by placing them under mathematical laws of mass and motion. This epistemological framework creates the standard picture of the human being as *Körper* in biomedicine, a discrete, causally determined physical substance that is, as Gadamer writes, "readily susceptible to objectification and the processes of measurement" (1996, 134). This is the decontextualized object that the psychiatrist encounters in the clinic: a set of data points waiting to be quantified using the taxonomic instruments of the DSM. To objectify the individual in the clinical setting, then, is simply *to measure* it, and the various affective, cognitive, and behavioral dysfunctions characteristic of mental illness are classified and subsumed under the general laws of quantification. The individual, on this view, is reduced to numeral data.

Obviously, what is missing from this objectifying picture is the human body *as it is lived*. Again, *Leib* is not a reference to an objectively present corporeal thing, but to *one's own* experiences, feelings, and perceptions as they are expressed, lived, and made intelligible within the context of a lifeworld. And I can never methodologically detach or disengage myself from my own body because it is already mediating how I encounter and make sense of things in everyday life. In this regard, my body exhibits a tacit practical knowledge (or know-how) shaped by the fact that I am structurally bound up in the meanings of a particular historical context. And this practical enmeshment reveals there is no Cartesian separation between mind and body or self and world. My embodied existence is, in short, a situated, self-interpreting site of meaning. In this view, the traditional account of the theoretical subject set over and against objects is itself derivative and parasitic on a more primordial phenomenon, namely the embodied practical knowledge of everyday life. For Dilthey, the situated complexity and incompleteness of our experience means that it can never be captured with the precision and exactness of mathematical laws. The interpretive study of humans, therefore, requires its own epistemological approach, a "human science," or *Geisteswissenschaft*, that takes as its object our own situated know-how, a form of knowledge that extends not only to everyday practices but also to human phenomena more generally, from cultural institutions and artifacts to languages, historical events, and works of art.

One of the signature contributions of Dilthey's account of the human sciences in this regard is the recognition that our embodied practices are best understood not in terms of inner mental states but as a spontaneous "expression" (*Ausdruck*) reflective of a shared context or atmosphere of meaning, and it is on the basis of dwelling in these atmospheres that we come to interpret and understand who we are and what is significant in our lives. As Dilthey explains:

We live in this atmosphere [of intelligibility]; it constantly surrounds us. We are immersed in it. Everywhere we are at home in this historical and intelligible world, we understand the sense and meaning [*Sinn und Bedeutung*] of all of it; we are interwoven into these shared understandings. (1958, 147)

In this view, the crisp, precise movements and emotionally detached ways of speaking that the psychiatrist embodies in the clinic are expressive of a particular context of meaning, and the psychiatrist understands who he or she is by expressing the mannerisms and gestures relevant to this context. The upshot is that the dispassionate attitude of the psychiatrist is not value neutral at all; it is, rather, a purposive and value-laden practice or way of life embedded in a world, one that identifies detachment and objectivity as valuable because it is the default standpoint for genuine knowledge.

From the perspective of epistemological hermeneutics, then, to understand or have knowledge of human experience is to have some understanding of the socio-historical conditions or meaning-structures that shape our experiences and make them intelligible. But there is a fundamental incompleteness or circularity to this kind of epistemology because any account of human experience is already distorted by the contextual situation we are thrown into. Consequently, there can be no objective "view from nowhere" in the *Geisteswissenschaften* because we can understand and interpret human phenomena only from within our own limited and situated perspective. This means one of the conditions of being human is the fact that we are always bound up in our own interpretative situation, and there is no way to fully extricate ourselves from it by means of methodological detachment, because as we now see, the value detachment is itself historically situated. Recognizing that when psychiatry employs the epistemology of the natural sciences it invariably regards the patient as a decontextualized object, we can now turn our attention to ontological hermeneutics, to the existence or *way of being* of the self-interpreting subject.

Paul Ricoeur describes the transition from epistemological to ontological hermeneutics in terms of "[digging] beneath the epistemological enterprise itself, in order to uncover its ontological conditions" (1981, 53).[2] The idea here is that a special kind of inquiry needs to take place, one that is prior to any theory of knowledge, and this inquiry concerns the existence or way of being of the entity that already interprets and understands the world. Hermeneutics is therefore not "a reflection on the human sciences, but an explication of the ontological ground upon which these sciences can be construed" (Ricoeur 1981, 55). Heidegger pioneers the conception of ontological hermeneutics in *Being and Time* by forwarding the idea that human existence is not a substance—an immaterial mind, a causally determined body, or some combination of the two—but the interpretive activity of existence itself. Thus, "man's 'substance' is not spirit as a synthesis of mind and body; it is rather *existence*" (BT, 117). Beginning with an analysis of human life as it is lived in ordinary situations, Heidegger shows that in the mundane activities of handling equipment, interacting with others, and fulfilling workaday obligations, we already embody a unique capacity for self-understanding, what he calls an "average and vague understanding of being" (*durchschnittliche und vage Seinsverständnis*). This means that in the midst of everyday life, we embody a tacit "home-like" (*heimelig*) familiarity with things, a familiarity that reveals the extent to which we are already connected with and concerned about the world and our place in it and that, through this connection, "[our] being is an *issue* for [us]" (BT, 12).

Heidegger captures this background familiarity with his famous account of "equipment" (*Zeug*) in *Being and Time*. By arguing that humans are already enmeshed in contexts of meaning and express a tacit understanding of how to handle and negotiate these contexts, he radically dismantles the Cartesian picture of the self as a cognizing subject. The human being is no longer viewed as a disembodied mind trying to gain knowledge of objects but as an embodied agent that skillfully uses tools and engages with others in a way that can never be made theoretically explicit. Using the analogy of hammering in the workshop, Heidegger shows that we understand the hammer only in relation to other tools such as nails, screws, and boards, as well as goal-directed projects like building a desk or shingling a roof. The idea here is that tools are intelligible or make sense only in relation to holistic practical contexts; a tool always "belongs to other equipment. [Thus], taken strictly, there 'is' no such thing as an equipment" (BT, 68). This means a tool reveals itself as intelligible for us only in terms of its contextual interdependence and because we already understand and are familiar with the context as a whole. And our understanding of a tool manifests itself not by means of any theoretical examination of its properties but by mindlessly "seiz[ing] hold of it and us[ing] it" (BT, 69). The hammer, in this case, reveals itself to me *as a hammer* in the serviceable act of hammering. Indeed, we are not thematically aware of the tool as an object separate from us in the course of everyday life. We are involved and bound up in the equipmental context to such an extent that the tool disappears or "withdraws" (*zurückzuziehen*) from our cognitive awareness. It is only when we take a deliberate stance of reflective detachment or when it is broken and unusable that the tool reveals itself to us as an object. Heidegger's point here is that the objectifying view that serves as the methodological benchmark of the *Naturwissenschaften* is actually parasitic on the preobjective handiness and familiarity of everyday life. And we can take this workshop analogy and apply it to the phenomenon of mental illness.

THE HERMENEUTICS OF MENTAL ILLNESS

In the same way equipment is already employed in serviceable tasks, so too are our bodies, as my hand, for instance, mindlessly reaches for the car keys, opens the door, or picks up the cell phone. Indeed, Heidegger traces the roots of the word "organ" back to the Greek *organon*, which literally means tool or instrument. Thus, "the [bodily] organ is a *Werkzeug*, a working instrument" (FCM, 213). And like the tool, my hand is also connected to a larger totality, to the shoulder, chest, torso, and my entire perceptual field, and it disappears or withdraws from my awareness in the course of my purposive activities (cf. Cerbone 2000). As we saw earlier, when things are functioning smoothly, my body is seamlessly enmeshed in a context of meaning and already understands how to maneuver through and handle this context. This embodied familiarity has little to do with inner cognitions that accurately represent outer objects. Being-in-the-world dissolves the inner/outer distinction altogether. I comprehend the meaning of things not by examining the content of my mind but by affectively grasping the whole horizon or experiential field I am involved in, and this understanding emerges incrementally through a process of acculturation, a contextual immersion that begins in early childhood. As Dilthey explains:

> Before the child learns to speak, it is already wholly immersed in a medium of commonalities. The child only learns to understand the gestures and facial expressions, movements and explanations, words and sentences, because it constantly encounters them as the same in the same relation to what they mean and express. Thus the individual becomes oriented in the world. (2002, 229–30)

Gadamer will refer to this background competence in terms of "health" (*Gesundheit*), and it is characterized by the forgetfulness of oneself as one disappears into the practical flow of everyday life. The enigma of health, then, is its own concealment or "hiddenness" (*Verborgenheit*); it is an embodied, rhythmic equilibrium that remains "constantly hidden from us" (1996, 112).

Health is not a condition determined by the absence of pain or the proper functioning of bodily organs and nervous systems. It is "a condition of being involved, of being-in-the-world, of being together with one's fellow human beings, of active and rewarding engagement in one's everyday tasks" (Gadamer 1996, 113). Absorbed in this state of balanced engagement, there is a tacit sense of well-being, where I feel comfortable and "at home" in the world. In episodes of mental illness, this sense of feeling connected and at home is replaced with the feeling of uncanniness. In this state, things that used to be familiar and comforting become unintelligible and strange. The taken-for-granted coherence and intelligibility of the world becomes a disorienting, alienating, even hostile place. Understood this way, *my* world is replaced with *the* world. Writer Tom Spanbauer captures this sense of anxiety in the following way.

> [In anxiety] things in the world are just things. Your house, table, your notebook, your computer, your bed, your toothbrush. Your clothes, your shoes, your socks, your car. Food. They have a life of their own unconnected to you. It's as if you're already dead and the world does not recognize you. And something even more. Because the things in the world don't recognize you, because your world isn't *your* world any more, it's just *the* world, instead of the familiar connections, you feel the empty place where you used to be connected, and without that connection, the way you're floating, things appear to you as having an energy barrier around them. And the energy of that barrier is a whole new weird deep anxiety. (2013, 293)

In order to empathically enter into Spanbaeur's experience, the psychiatrist needs to make a distinction between what is scientifically "explainable" (*erklärbar*) about the cause of his anxiety from what is "understandable" (*verständlich*) about the experience itself.

Articulating the distinction between "explanation" (*Erklärung*) and "understanding" (*Verstehen*) is key to the practice of hermeneutic psychiatry. As early as 1913, in his masterwork *General Psychopathology,* Karl Jaspers introduced this difference, making it clear that the method of explanation approaches the phenomenon of mental illness in a similar way that the physicist studies and quantifies the causal relations of matter. Thus, in psychopathology, the psychiatrist tries to identify particular causal connections by examining, for instance, brain structure, measuring heart and respiration rates, reviewing dietary and sleep patterns, or analyzing heredity. Here, the psychiatrist remains at a cool distance, regarding the patient as an object. Contrast this with understanding, where, in Jaspers's words, "we sink ourselves into the psychic situation [of the patient] and *understand genetically by empathy* how one psychic event emerges from another" (1997, 301). Rather than reducing the patient to a set of data points and forcing that data into the pre-established categories of the DSM, the psychiatrist is called to open an empathic dialogue with the patient in an attempt to bring to light the complex web of meanings that allow the patient to understand him or herself. In this dialogue, the psychiatrist recognizes that she does not occupy an objective or neutral standpoint. The psychiatrist's interpretation is always corrupted by a "fore-structure" (*Vor-Struktur*) of assumptions and biases to which she is obliged to be attentive. Gadamer explains that the kind of sensitivity necessary in hermeneutic dialogue

> involves neither "neutrality" with respect to content nor the extinction of one's self, but the foregrounding and appropriation of one's own fore-meanings and prejudices. The important thing is to be aware of one's own bias, so that the

[life-story] can present itself in all its otherness and thus assert its own truth against one's own fore-meanings. (1994, 269)

For Gadamer, this "requires remaining open to the meaning of the other person's [experience]" (1994, 268), where the psychiatrist lets the patient's story unfold while realizing that—because she too is shaped by prejudices— any interpretation of this story will remain ambiguous and open-ended.

In this way, the psychiatrist does not determine the meaning of the patient's agitation or despondency by dispassionately reflecting on his or her symptoms. The meaning is determined, rather, by the shared cultural arrangements and social patterns that the patient is already immersed in and familiar with. The psychiatrist begins to understand the patient's experience by sinking into the web of meanings that constitute the patient's world. Responding to vague complaints of feeling "depressed" or "empty," for example, the psychiatrist may begin by asking simple questions about events in the patient's life that might be significant. Has he or she recently divorced, moved to another city, lost a job, or filed for bankruptcy?[3] By following the thread of these initial questions and letting the patient describe his or her situation, the psychiatrist can begin to sink into the patient's world, to understand—in a nonobjectifying way—what events, values, and commitments matter to him or her. From here, the questioning can move more broadly and deeply into the meaning-structures of modernity itself and what it means to dwell in and be shaped by these structures. This can involve, among other things, an examination of the loss of community and belongingness in the age of Facebook and Instagram; the spiritual emptiness and erosion of moral absolutes in an increasingly secular society; the boredom, crass materialism, and ecological degradation of mass consumerism; or the forlornness that comes from seeing ourselves as masterful individuals rather than vulnerable beings who are mutually dependent on each other. Here the patient's experience of emptiness and alienation cannot be reduced to chemical imbalances in the brain because it emerges out of being-in-the-world itself. Consider the case of Alec.

> Alec is forty-two, single, and for most of his life has felt lonely and alienated. He has never cared much about politics, considers himself an agnostic, and has never found a hobby or interest he would want to pursue consistently. He says he does not think he really has a self at all. He has had two stints of psychotherapy; both ended inconclusively, leaving him still with chronic, low-grade depression. Nowadays he is feeling a little better about himself. He has started attending a local meeting of Adult Children of Alcoholics. People at the meetings seem to understand and validate his pain; he is making friends there and believes he "belongs" for the first time since he left the military. But he confesses to his therapist that he feels "sort of squirrelly" about it because he is not an adult child of an alcoholic. He is faking the pathological label in order

to be accepted by the community, and he is not too sure he really buys into
their twelve-step ideology either. (Elliott 2016, 127–28)

From the perspective of hermeneutic psychiatry, the condition Alec is suffering from is not inside his head, the result of low levels of serotonin or
dopamine. Rather, it emerges from his inability to fit or cohere with the
broader social expectations and meaning-structures of the world he has been
thrown into.[4] The aim, then, is not simply to eradicate Alec's existential pain
with Prozac but to situate it and come to grips with the socio-historical
sources that made it possible. The hope is that this kind of contextual interro-
gation will ultimately move Alec in the direction of "self-understanding"
(*Sichverstehen*). A dialogical exchange of this kind enables the psychiatrist
to see Alec as more than a natural object and that any interpretation of Alec's
suffering is irreducibly ambiguous and undetermined.[5] It is a mistake, then,
to think the psychiatrist is simply "re-creating" the patient's experience.
"Questions always bring out the undetermined possibilities of a thing,"
writes Gadamer. "This is the reason why understanding is always more than
merely re-creating someone else's meaning. Questioning opens up possibilities of meaning, and thus what is meaningful passes into one's own thinking
on the subject" (1994, 375).

In hermeneutic therapy, both psychiatrist and patient lose themselves in
the dialogical "to and fro" as they move toward self-understanding. By remaining flexible and sensitive to the alterity of the patient's experience, the
psychiatrist temporarily suspends the reductive nosology of the DSM and
remains open, *letting* the patient's situated experience emerge and reveal
itself on its own terms. In this hermeneutic openness, the psychiatrist is able
"to *hear* what the other is saying" (Gadamer 1994, 316). The possibility of
hearing the patient is all too often stifled by the reductive framework of
biopsychiatry, with the result that "instead of learning to look for illness in
the eyes of the patient or to listen for it in the patient's voice, [the psychi-
atrist] tries to read the data off of diagnostic instruments" (Gadamer 1996,
98). From a hermeneutic perspective, the truth of mental illness is not to be
found in the measurement of objective data, but in what Gadamer calls the
"in-between," where two horizons of understanding—that of the psychiatrist
and of the patient—fuse together in the flow of dialogue and are both transformed by the event. In these instances, hermeneutic dialogue serves a
"bridging" (*Überbrückung*) function between psychiatrist and patient, providing "due recognition to the fact that what is involved is always a relationship between two human beings" (Gadamer 1996, 171).

We can see, then, that it is more accurate and ultimately more productive
to interpret psychiatry as a "human science" (*Geisteswissenschaft*) rather
than a "natural science" (*Naturwissenschaft*). As a human science, hermeneutic psychiatry reminds us that our being-in-the-world cannot be collapsed

into a technical procedure or method that, if followed correctly, can arrive at some transhistorical truth about mental illness. To bring the human being back into psychiatric treatment, the hegemony of *methodologism* and technical expertise needs to be challenged. Again, I am not suggesting that the perspective of natural science is the problem. The problem, as Heidegger makes clear, is "the victory of the *scientific method* over science" (ZS1, 134), that is, of uncritically applying a genetic-causal explanation to all things, including the thrown finitude of human existence. The strict emphasis on method that biopsychiatry abides by continues to cut the psychiatrist away from a deeper sense of truth, the truth of the patient's own self-understanding, an understanding that always "transcends the sphere of the scientific method" (Gadamer 1994, xxii). As a human science, psychiatry would, of course, not rule out of the use of medication or even the nosology of the DSM, but the first priority would always be to remain attentive to the patient's life and the ways in which it is inextricably bound to the world. This is why psychiatry is more akin to an interpretative art than it is to an applied science and why the psychiatrist always "needs more than just scientific and technical knowledge and professional experience" (Gadamer 1996, 172).

Having laid out the conceptual foundations and clinical value of hermeneutic psychiatry, we can now broaden our discussion and explore the ways in which the meaning-structures of modernity tacitly construct standards of normalcy and that failing to conform to these standards often results in a psychiatric diagnosis. From a hermeneutic perspective, then, the way in which American psychiatry has medicalized different aspects of the human condition reveals more about *who we are* and *what matters* to us in the current age than it does about any chemical imbalance in the brain. We will begin by exploring the socio-historical conditions that shaped and normalized the American self as a gregarious and assertive extrovert and how privileging the values of extroversion invariably diminishes those of introversion, reflection, and sensitivity. Normalizing extroversion as the cultural default for health and success in America has made it possible to pathologize shyness, laying the groundwork for the introduction of a new diagnostic category in the DSM, social anxiety disorder (or social phobia), opening the floodgates for various medications and technologies to treat it, and creating a situation where being confident and self-promoting has become compulsory.

NOTES

1. Medard Boss describes the difficulty of bringing this kind of hermeneutic awareness into mainstream clinical practice because of how it undermines the scientific and technological prejudices that physicians are habituated into. "Many medical people (*Mediziner*) remain suspicious. Those who have been hardened by a purely scientific, materialistic positivistic way of thinking do so with good reason. The phenomenological approach threatens this claim to

absoluteness regarding man. Moreover, given the trends of our technical age they feel more committed than ever to hold onto them under any circumstances" (Boss 2019, 191).

2. Here, I am indebted to numerous conversations with Charles Guignon over the years on the nature of hermeneutic philosophy. For a rich and comprehensive account of the distinction between epistemological and ontological hermeneutics, see Guignon (1999).

3. Bracken and Thomas describe how psychiatry objectifies the patient's experience in the following way: "In psychiatry, a person might complain of feeling 'empty,' 'without direction,' 'fed up,' or simply 'miserable.' These feelings are often bound up with such things as unhappy relationships, difficult work situations, or physical health. In the psychiatrist's formulation, these feelings become 'dysphoric mood' or 'symptoms of depression.' Painful thoughts about the possibility of ending one's life, with all of the cultural, religious, personal and family implications and nuances that such thoughts invariably bring to the fore, become simply 'suicidal ideation'" (2005, 108).

4. This is why mental distress is embodied and understood differently in different cultures and historical epochs. Psychiatrist Thomas Fuchs (2013b), for example, points out that in some cultures, depression is not experienced as an "affective mood disorder" as the DSM claims. Rather, it is experienced solely in terms of somatic complaints of fatigue and exhaustion with little or no awareness of the sadness, guilt, or anxiety that accompany the Western diagnosis.

5. This explains Gadamer's claim that: "[We are] in a mysterious way unknown to ourselves and to others. As a public person, as a neighbor, in the family and at work, each one of us responds to innumerable and incalculable effects and influences, burdens and problems" (1996, 164).

Chapter Six

Situating Shyness

Extrovert Privilege and American Selfhood

In 1846, Kierkegaard introduced a scathing indictment of the present age, describing the modern self as a gregarious socializer, obsessed with gossip and constantly on the lookout for novelty and distraction. "If I tried to imagine [such a person]," writes Kierkegaard, "I should think of . . . a large well-fed figure, suffering from boredom, looking only for the sensual intoxication of laughter" (1973, 267). Kierkegaard is mocking what he sees as the "leveling" quality of mass societies, where people are secure and happy when they do what everyone else does, where "everyone is reduced to a common denominator" (1973, 269). The consequence, for Kierkegaard, is to conform to expectations of sociability, where being the life of the party is praised and solitary and sensitive types are stigmatized as abnormal, even criminal. In *Sickness unto Death* (1849), he writes:

> In the constant sociability of our age people shudder at solitude to such a degree that they know no other use to put it to but (oh, admirable epigram!) as a punishment for criminals. But after all it is a fact that in our age it is a crime to have spirit, so it is natural that such people, the lovers of solitude, are included in the same class with criminals. (1973, 363)

Kierkegaard struggled to reconcile the public expectation for extroversion with his own quiet and reflective disposition. Putting on the mask of sociability at parties was almost unbearable. In his journal, he confesses:

> I have just returned from a party of which I was the life and soul; wit poured from my lips, everyone laughed and admired me—but I went away—and the

77

dash should be as long as the earth's orbit—and I wanted to shoot myself. (1973, 363)

Kierkegaard was deeply suspicious of the public's reluctance to accept dispositions that do not conform to standards of normalcy. If the core principle of modern democracy is that "everyone is equal to everyone else," then there is little room for the solitary, sensitive, and introverted individual. Although his polemics against compulsory extroversion are a bit extreme, Kierkegaard's critique has taken on new meaning in America today as shyness—understood minimally as a kind of behavioral inhibition combined with anxiety or distress in social or performance situations—is not only interpreted as abnormal, it has been pathologized as a mental disorder. By the early 1990s, *Psychology Today* had dubbed shyness the "disorder of the decade," and an article in the *Harvard Review of Psychiatry* referred to it as "the third-most-common psychiatric disorder, behind only major depressive disorder and alcohol dependence" (Lane 2007, 5; Rettew 2000, 2985). Pathological shyness, now referred to as social anxiety disorder (or social phobia), purportedly affects a staggering 13 percent of the population, one person in eight (Horwitz 2002, 95; McDaniel 2003, 9; Cottle 1999).

As early as the 1960s, critics such as R. D. Laing, Thomas Szasz, Ervin Goffman, and Michel Foucault began attacking psychiatry's effort to medicalize the human condition. And as we saw in chapter 1, this turn toward medicalization has reached a fever pitch in recent decades as the APA adopted an increasingly reductive interpretation of mental illness and became inextricably tied to the pharmaceutical industry in terms of funding and research. The result is the proliferation of quick-fix pharmaceuticals to treat a wide range of behaviors and affects. This pattern has become particularly problematic in situations like shyness, because it refers to a dispositional cluster—including quietness, sensitivity, reflection, and humility—that has, in the context of our own history, been regarded as valuable and even praiseworthy. These aspects of character, especially in post–World War II America, have been replaced with what Susan Cain (2012) calls the "Extrovert Ideal," one that privileges those who are outgoing, assertive, and self-expressive. To this end, I want to suggest the psychiatric effort to pathologize shyness reveals more about the way we understand and interpret the self in late modernity than it does about chemical imbalances.

By decontextualizing shyness and treating it as a discrete medical entity, American psychiatry is unable to engage the question of how and why the Extrovert Ideal emerged and matters to us in the first place. This is why the hermeneutic approach is so helpful. By interpreting human existence in terms of being-in-the-world, the clinician regards the patient not as an isolated set of symptoms but as a situated existence that is already engaged in a world. In this regard, hermeneutic psychiatry opens up the possibility for clinicians to contextualize affects and behavior, revealing the extent to which they are historically embedded and how we unconsciously enact and reify them in everyday life. This analysis sheds light on the kind of compulsory extroversion that exists in America today, where being outgoing and self-promoting is not something we necessarily want to do but *have to do* in order to succeed in our hyperindividualistic and competitive society. But before beginning this hermeneutic analysis, we have to put the recent medicalization of shyness in context.

THE DSM AND THE MEDICALIZATION OF SHYNESS

As we saw in chapter 1, the turn toward medicalization in American psychiatry can be attributed largely to a fundamental change in the way mental illnesses were diagnosed, a change that culminated in 1980 with the publication of the DSM-III. The DSM-III became the so-called "bible of psychiatry," representing a return to the objectivity and neutrality of empirical science and a rejection of the ideology and diagnostic sloppiness that plagued psychodynamic (or psychoanalytic) theory. One of the ways to address the diagnostic problem was to eliminate the vague, ideologically loaded term "neuroses"—which tended to normalize pathology and blur the distinction between ordinary behavior and illness—and replace it with a more neutral term that signified a genuine medical condition, "disorder" (Horwitz 2002, 72; Horwitz and Wakefield 2007, 15). As a result of this shift, the broad classification of "anxiety neurosis" that was so fundamental to psychoanalysis was broken into seven new disorders: agoraphobia, panic disorder, post-traumatic stress disorder, obsessive compulsive disorder, generalized anxiety disorder, simple phobia, and social anxiety disorder (or social phobia) (Lane 2007).

This new system of classification was modeled after the natural sciences. To this end, it explicitly rejected all theoretical assumptions about the etiology of mental disorders, offering only a "descriptive approach [and] attempt[ed] to be neutral with respect to theories of etiology" (APA 1994, xvii-xviii). Given its aim of etiological neutrality, the DSM taskforce focused exclusively on carving up psychopathologies on the basis of symptoms, and new disorders were introduced based solely on the presence and frequency of symptoms. But this empirical approach revealed a serious problem because the prevalence of a given disorder could be easily manipulated by slight changes to the diagnostic criterion itself. This was especially true in the case of social phobia.

The DSM-I and II did not mention social phobia, and when it finally did appear in the DSM-III, it was regarded as a "disorder [that] is apparently relatively rare" (APA 1980, 228; Cottle 1999). But by the time the DSM-IV was published in 1994, social phobia had gone from a rare disorder, affecting only 2.75 percent of the population, into a raging epidemic affecting a staggering 13 percent (Cottle 1999; Horwitz 2002). Psychiatrist Peter Kramer (1997) explains this dramatic change in terms of what he calls, "diagnostic bracket creep," a reference to how slight changes in the criteria used to identify disorders can determine how many people actually have the disorder (Lane 2007, 78). The way the definition of social phobia changed over the years is evidence of the disorder's plasticity. In 1980, for example, the DSM-III defined social anxiety disorder as:

> A persistent, irrational fear of, and compelling desire to avoid, situations in which the individual may be exposed to scrutiny by others and fears that he or she may act in a way that will be humiliating or embarrassing. (APA 1980, 228)

When the DSM-IV appeared in 1994, the definition changed to:

> A marked and persistent fear of one or more social or performance situations in which the person is exposed to unfamiliar people or to possible scrutiny by others. The individual fears that he or she will act in a way (or show anxiety symptoms) that will be humiliating or embarrassing. (APA 1994, 456)

And with the publication of the DSM-V in 2013, examples of phobia-triggering situations were added to the definition, including: "social interactions (e.g., having a conversation, meeting unfamiliar people), being observed (e.g., eating or drinking), and performing in front of others (e.g., giving a speech)" (APA 2013, 202). With these subtle changes in definition, social phobia no longer involved a "compelling desire to avoid" situations of social exposure, a phrase that captured the intensity of the anxiety insofar as one might avoid the situation altogether (Cottle 1999; Horwitz 2002; McDaniel 2003). The experience of "marked and persistent fear" by an individual in *any* social or performance situation would now be sufficient for a diagnosis. As a result, the numbers of Americans suffering from social phobia skyrocketed, and it became increasingly difficult to distinguish ordinary shyness from a full-blown mental disorder.[1]

Although the DSM tries to distinguish ordinary shyness from social phobia by claiming, for instance, that only the latter "leads to clinically significant distress or impairment" (APA 2013, 203), this distinction is not at all clear. Am I suffering from a mental illness, for instance, if I am significantly impaired or distressed before giving an important public speech? Not necessarily. This could be regarded as a normal reaction to a rare, high-pressure situation. However, what if giving speeches is part of my job, but my distress is so severe that I am unable to do so and, consequently, may get fired? This is obviously a more serious situation that may require some sort of intervention, but it still does not constitute a medical condition. Rather, it may be a reflection of an individual being unable to cope with the unique demands of contemporary working life. The problem with the DSM, then, is that it is unable to situate individual symptoms within any kind of meaningful socio-historical context. I could be diagnosed in either case because the symptoms of social phobia, taken on their own, are sufficient for a diagnosis. This, of course, opened the door for a massive new market for antishyness medications. And in 1999, the FDA approved Paxil as the first antidepressant to be used specifically for social anxiety disorder, followed by massive advertising campaigns and advocacy groups touting the seriousness of the disorder as a severely underdiagnosed medical condition (Lane 2007, 104–138; Horwitz 2002, 95).[2]

Anticipating the publication of the DSM-III, a number of prominent American psychiatrists and psychologists, mindful of the fact that affects and behaviors are socially and culturally situated, expressed alarm at the impending medicalization of shyness. Christopher Lane (2007) documents this reaction, citing a 1978 memo to DSM-III architect Robert Spitzer by psychiatrist Joseph Finney, who points out that the medicalization of shyness reflected a "cultural prejudice in our diagnostic classification system. . . . Ours happens to be an extroverted culture, and so we tend to stigmatize introverts. . . . The opposite is true in Japan, where introverts are regarded as normal and extroverts are abnormal" (Lane 2007, 90).[3] Some psychiatrists even remarked on how the culture of psychiatry itself attracts a disproportionate number of introverted and social phobic personalities to the discipline. In a memo to Spitzer, psychologist Mary McCaulley writes, "It is ironic to me that DSM-III is being developed by two fields, psychiatry and psychology, where introverts appear to be in the majority. . . . On a more general level, I do not think that every human being needs to be classified under DSM-III. We have enough trouble correctly categorizing our [own] patients" (Lane 2007, 83). And psychiatrist Otto Allen Will echoed McCaulley's sentiments, objecting to Spitzer's classification of shyness because he would be inclined to pathologize *himself*. "In many ways," he remarks, "my own personality fits into the characterization of the new disorder" (Lane 2007, 78).[4]

Although the DSM taskforce acknowledges that "cultural meanings, habits, and traditions may also contribute to vulnerability and suffering" (APA 2013, 14), what is missing is a critical investigation into the meaning-structures of American culture itself and how these structures already shape the agenda of diagnostic psychiatry. This kind of hermeneutic inquiry serves a number of heuristic functions. First, it opens up the possibility for psychiatrists to question their uncritical reliance on the atomistic nosology of the DSM. Second, it reveals the extent to which standards of normalcy are not fixed and timeless but already shaped by the meanings of our own history and how these meanings tacitly inform clinical practice. And third, it allows psychiatry to broaden its conception of the self as a discrete set of symptoms. From the standpoint of hermeneutic psychiatry, the self is, first and foremost, an embodied agent thrown into a context of meanings. This reconfiguration of selfhood allows us to explore the possibility that social phobia may not indicate a pathology. Indeed, it may be an acceptable, even healthy, response to the relational tensions and upheavals of modern American life.

HERMENEUTIC PSYCHIATRY AND THE EXTROVERT IDEAL

As we have seen, to understand the self from a hermeneutic perspective is to understand the historical context that we are immersed in and familiar with. This is why Heidegger says, "To understand history cannot mean anything else than to understand ourselves" (PS, 7). This contextual familiarity suggests that humans already embody a prereflective understanding of what it means to be in everyday situations. As we go about our daily lives, things reveal themselves to us immediately and directly as value laden, as already saturated with significance. The meanings of things do not reside inside our minds or brains. They are, rather, enacted in our everyday practices as part of the historical background we grow into, and this shared background shapes in advance how we understand and make sense of things. What this suggests is that "history" (*Geschichte*) does not exist in the past as events that are external to us. History is always operating behind our backs, guiding any interpretation we can have of the world and ourselves and opening up possible ways for us to be in the future. In this sense, there is no way to extricate or free ourselves from the interpretations and meanings handed down by our forbearers. Heidegger explains:

> The everyday way in which things have been interpreted is one into which [human beings have] grown in the first instance, with never a possibility of extrication. In it, out of it, and against it, all genuine understanding, interpreting, and communicating, all re-discovering and appropriating anew, are performed. In no case is [a human being] untouched and unseduced by this way in which things have been interpreted. (BT, 169)

Hermeneutic psychiatry, then, illuminates the extent to which we unconsciously enact and construct the biases of our own tradition. In terms of understanding mental illness, it requires us to shift our attention from *what we are* as biochemical organisms to *how we are* as embodied agents in the world. It is only on the basis of the historically mediated structures of life that we can begin to understand or interpret ourselves *as* the kinds of people we are. With this in mind, we can turn to the question of why it is that Americans generally value the Extrovert Ideal and marginalize the shy.

To address this question, we have to first get a sense of the unique socio-historical upheavals that were emerging in America at the end of the nine-teenth century. Although in no way exhaustive, we can identify a number of overlapping factors that, taken together, began to unsettle the centuries-old values and meanings that shaped the premodern self. First, in the wake of growing industrialization, urbanization, and mass immigration, there was a dramatic loss of the close-knit bonds characteristic of rural and agrarian communities, resulting in an American existence that was increasingly mo-bile, complex, and alienating. Indeed, in 1840 only 8 percent of Americans lived in cities, but by 1920, more than a third of the population had migrated and became urbanites (Cain 2012). Second, the rise of scientism altered older understandings of our place in the world. The world was no longer regarded as an enchanted garden or "great chain of being" filled with divine purpose. The world had become, in Max Weber's words, "disenchanted," a mechanis-tic aggregate of valueless objects in causal interaction waiting to be manipu-lated and mastered by new technologies. Third, the moral tensions that arose from the institution of slavery, the Indian Wars, and, of course, the Civil War began to undermine the American belief in Manifest Destiny and the as-sumption of Anglo-Saxon superiority (Cushman 1995). The result was an emergent wave of moral anomie and confusion that crested with the mecha-nized horrors of the Great War and documented by the "Lost Generation" of American writers such as F. Scott Fitzgerald, Gertrude Stein, Ernest Heming-way, and T. S. Eliot. Fourth, the conception of the self as a masterful, indus-trious individual began to take hold. The Protestant emphasis on individual-ism, self-reliance, and the idea that "one exists for the sake of one's work alone" left an indelible stamp on American identity (Weber 1998, 70). This Protestant ethos corresponded to a new picture of society, where we no longer understood ourselves in terms of our place in a preordained natural order. Society, rather, came to be viewed as something artificial, an aggre-gate of individuals held together by instrumental business contracts and transactional exchanges. In this view, social life began to emerge as some-thing unnatural or "fake," where one is compelled to adopt a public persona or "mask" in order to negotiate an increasingly impersonal and alienating social order (Guignon 2004).

The combined effect of these overlapping historical events contributed to what Charles Taylor (2007) calls "the Great Disembedding." The result is a uniquely modern sense of self, where we no longer understand ourselves in terms of a transcendent moral order, where our acts and practices are mean-ingful to the extent that they are embedded in a context of shared rituals, institutions, and beliefs. The modern American has been uprooted from this thick moral framework and begins to interpret himself or herself as an indi-vidual, a masterful self-reliant ego. The consequence of this loss of commu-nity, family, and tradition was an increasingly fragmented, complex, and isolated existence embodied in growing feelings of anxiety, confusion, and, as we will see in the next chapter, a new condition of the nerves called "neurasthenia" (Beard 1881) or "Americanitis" (Knapp 1896) that was exploding into an epidemic.

Applying a hermeneutic critique, we can see how this historical uprooting resulted in a new configuration of the American self. By the end of the nineteenth century Americans were no longer shaped by the religious sense of "character," which involved submission to moral laws, duty, rejection of pride and self-congratulation, and a sense of humility. Though still highly individualistic, the self as an embodiment of a certain kind of Protestant character was replaced by a new quality: "personality." Americans were now concerned with how others perceived them, and advice manuals began to promote the individual's ability to be charming and magnetic, to stand out in a crowd and to be attractive to others. Victorian honor, manners, and reserve in public situations were no longer conducive to success in a rapidly changing capitalist economy. Philip Cushman explains:

> Capitalism was moving into a new phase of its history. An emphasis on hard work and honest labor was being replaced by an emphasis on sales and consumption of goods and services, predicated upon the effectiveness of a sales technique and/or the attractiveness of the individual salesperson. Personal magnetism replaced craftsmanship; technique replaced moral integrity. (1995, 65)

With the emergence of the cult of personality in this new transactional economy, the self was being tacitly reconfigured into an outgoing, assertive, and confident salesman, and those that could not live up to these social expectations would be deprived of wealth, professional and interpersonal success, and power.

Susan Cain (2012) documents how this cultural shift was evident with the rise of a new kind of self-help book pioneered by turn-of-the-century figures like Dale Carnegie in works such as *The Art of Public Speaking and Influencing Men* (1926) and the best-selling *How to Win Friends and Influence People* (1936) that promoted and cultivated the skills of the Extrovert Ideal. Carnegie tapped into the importance of self-presentation, confidence, and personal magnetism for success in modern deal making. And the advertising industry followed Carnegie's lead, moving from straightforward product announcements to personality-driven ads, where the product itself played a role in providing the consumer with the attractiveness, power, and confidence they needed to succeed. Cain points to a popular 1920s ad for Woodbury soap that reads: "All around the world people are judging you silently," and another by the Williams Shaving Cream Company that advises the consumer to "Let your face reflect confidence, not worry! It's the 'look' of you by which you are judged most often" (Cain 2012, 24). She goes on to document how, by midcentury, the Extrovert Ideal had found its way into the admissions offices of America's most elite universities where, for example, Harvard provost Paul Buck made it clear that he would reject "sensitive, neurotic, and overly intellectual" applicants in favor of young men who embodied a "healthy extroverted" disposition, and Yale president Alfred Whitney Griswold declared that the ideal student is not a "beetle-browed, highly specialized intellectual, but a well rounded man" (Cain 2012, 28).

This masterful, assertive, extroverted self reached full maturity in the post–World War II economy. It was at this time—in the age of credit cards, ubiquitous advertising, television, and the ceaseless production and consumption of nonessential and quickly obsolete products—that middle-class Americans began to embrace this new set of social expectations, and the self emerged as a confident and optimistic consumer and salesperson. But underneath this façade of self-confidence was a growing sense of insecurity and unease, and countless Americans began to crack under the pressure. Scott Stossel (2015) describes how the pharmaceutical industry quickly stepped in to meet the challenge. By 1955, the drug company Carter-Wallace had released a new brand of tranquilizer, the benzodiazepine Miltown, to soothe those struggling to keep up with the Extrovert Ideal. A year later, one in every twenty Americans had taken it. In 1960, Hoffman-La Roche pharmaceutics released a similar drug, Librium, for the "treatment of common anxieties and tension," and within months, its sales had eclipsed those of Miltown. It remained the best-selling drug in America until 1969. And in 1970, Hoffman-La Roche released the blockbuster benzodiazepine Valium. By 1975, one in every five women and one in every thirteen men in America had taken Miltown, Librium, or Valium, and one study revealed that nearly 20 percent of American *physicians* were regularly taking benzodiazepines in the 1970s. These drugs had become, at the time, the biggest commercial success in the history of the American pharmaceutical industry, and when Upjohn pharmaceutics introduced the powerful, fast-acting benzodiazepine Xanax in 1986, it quickly became the best-selling drug in American history (Stossel 2015, 192–197).

In the hermeneutic reading, this emergent anxiety and the various medications created to treat it are bound up in the context of modernity itself, one where we no longer see ourselves rooted to a communal order that provides an enduring moral framework and stable social roles. The self of late modernity is increasingly unmoored and anonymous. In today's neoliberal economy, we are forced into being self-sufficient and self-creating as we careen from one career, relationship, and geographical location to another. The result, according to social theorists like Anthony Giddens (1991) and Ulrich Beck (1992), is a feeling of exposure and risk as we constantly encounter unfamiliar people and places and a pervasive fear at being evaluated and judged by others. This creates an intensified sense of self-consciousness and a wariness regarding how to behave in public. But with this existential uncertainty, there is a social expectation to be assertive and confident, and we are compelled to conform to these expectations, to continually rehearse and prepare for public judgments in order to demonstrate that we can handle today's fragmented and rapidly changing social environments.

Perhaps no writer captured the "age of anxiety" in post–World War II America better than Richard Yates. In his novel *Revolutionary Road* (1961), the protagonists Frank and April Wheeler are in a constant state of self-evaluation, measuring their lives against those portrayed in advertising fantasies, television programs, and movies, worrying about how others see them and obsessed with their social status. As critic Stewart O'Nan (1999) remarks: "It's as if they're playing at their roles of man and woman, husband and wife, mother and father, terrified they'll blow their lines." Frank and April embody a uniquely American form of social phobia, where assertiveness and self-confidence is, in large part, an illusion employed to cover over an underlying anxiety because we no longer have a cohesive and stable sense of *who we are*. This, in turn, creates a kind of reflexive feedback loop whereby we constantly try to reassert ourselves as confident, charming, and sociable in order to compensate for our own insecurity. And the distress of those who are already temperamentally quiet, sensitive, and introverted is exacerbated because they are unable to measure up to social expectations. The outcome begins to look a lot like Kierkegaard's conception of leveling, where today an entire industry of assertiveness clinics, anxiety medications, self-help books, and pop psychology has been created to pull the shy out of their reclusive shells so they can be resocialized into the norm, into fascinating, emotionally expressive people-persons. Among the most popular of these emergent technologies today is Landmark Forum, the legacy of Werner Erhard's program, Erhard Seminar Training (or "est"), which flourished alongside places like Esalen during California's booming human potential movement in the 1960s and '70s. According to its website, participants in the Forum today pay upwards of one thousand dollars per session to learn how to self-actualize as an effective and masterful individual and to "gain the freedom to be at ease in any circumstance" (Cederström 2018, 85).

An obvious consequence of this kind of compulsory extroversion and the flattening of emotional life in America is that the positive aspects of shyness, such as seriousness, sensitivity, reflection, modesty, and listening, are diminished. From a hermeneutic perspective, however, a deeper problem emerges. This involves forgetting the extent to which our self-understanding is dependent on the ways in which we are thrown into webs of meaning. The value of a hermeneutic approach for clinicians is that is reveals how social norms are always embedded in these unfolding historical webs. To this end, it will always emphasize situated "understanding" (*Verstehen*) over causal "explanation" (*Erklärung*). It may be true that the naturalistic ontology uncritically embraced by American psychiatry will one day be able to explain the mechanistic functioning of neurotransmitters and their relationship to subjective experience, but it will always fail to give an account of the world, to the relational background that shapes how behaviors and dispositions matter to us in the first place. As Heidegger reminds us, "even if an ontology should itself succeed in explicating the being of nature in the very purest manner . . . which mathematical natural science provides, it will never reach the phenomenon that is 'world'" (BT, 92, my emphasis).

Again, the aim of hermeneutic psychiatry is not to address the biochemical mechanisms of an organism but to enter into the historical structures that make any understanding or meaning-formation possible. To understand the sufferer, then, is to understand him or her as a "historical" (*geschichtlich*) being bound to the world, not an organism or personality apart from it. This approach helps dismantle the increasingly widespread view held by antipsychiatry critics that the medicalization of American life is largely a product of collusion and profiteering between medical professionals and Big Pharma (e.g., Glenmullen 2001; Healy 2006; Lane 2007). We now see that before clinicians and pharmaceutical conglomerates can profit from medicalizing conditions like shyness, webs of meaning are already working behind our backs, informing what will count for us as normal or abnormal.[5] The late modern American values of sociability, emotional expressiveness, and assertiveness are not essential traits of normalcy arrived at through some detached diagnostic procedure; they are already affected by history. This is why, in Gadamer's words, "an awareness of social norms, as well as corresponding forms of behavior on the part of society as a whole, [will] always contribute to the definition . . . of [mental] illness, and so render it problematic" (Gadamer 1996, 169, my emphasis).

By neglecting our hermeneutic situation, clinicians will continue to perpetuate the ideology of the status quo. And this lack of awareness simply reifies the values of the Extrovert Ideal, magnifying the spread of social phobia as we promote and market ourselves as confident and masterful but simultaneously worry about being judged by others. Caught up in the norms of late modernity, we are unable to see social phobia from a historical perspective, as a normal, perhaps even healthy, response to an increasingly isolated, fragmented, and overwhelming existence. In this regard, my argument does not line up with antipsychiatry critics who argue psychiatric medications are scientifically worthless and socially harmful. On the contrary, I maintain that there is in fact a marked increase in social anxiety in America and that medications are helpful to millions, but not because the sufferer has a medical condition. They are helpful, in this case, because they allow the sufferer to cope with compulsory extroversion. But by medicalizing shyness, American psychiatry continues to produce a more assertive, competitive, and isolated self and paradoxically exacerbates the experience of anxiety. It is, in short, constructing and perpetuating the very pathology it is seeking to treat.

We can now turn our hermeneutic attention to the broader role that language plays in psychiatric diagnosis, and how the meanings of diagnostic terms change on the basis of the shifts and upheavals of our historical situation. By focusing on the late-nineteenth-century diagnosis of neurasthenia in America and its reincarnation today in functional somatic conditions like fibromyalgia and chronic fatigue syndrome, the aim is to show how the discourses of biology and naturalism have come to dominate our interpretation of psychosomatic conditions and explore the cultural motivation for interpreting them in medical rather than in psychiatric terms. Hermeneutic psychiatry not only exposes the limits of naturalism as the default setting for any account of psychosomatic suffering, it also illuminates the extent to which this kind of suffering may be a uniquely modern ailment embedded in a particular context of meaning that determines how we experience and make sense of our pain and exhaustion. Based on this view, conditions like fibromyalgia and chronic fatigue syndrome may not be the result of some unknown pathology but of simply existing in the modern world itself.

NOTES

1. Allan Horwitz points out how this became particularly evident in a National Co-Morbidity Survey (NCS) in the early 1990s in which people received a diagnosis of social phobia if they experienced marked distress in any number of ordinary situations: "public speaking, feeling foolish when speaking to others, writing while someone watches, or talking in front of small groups" (2002, 95).

2. This pattern of medicalization is especially troubling when it comes to shyness because one can obviously be healthy, contented, high functioning, *and* shy. In response to the DSM's new classification, for example, clinical psychologist Naomi Quenk writes, "It is a gross disservice to the valuable and well-functioning introverts in our society. . . . [I am] greatly concerned to have a pathological label attached to their normal and healthy attitude. It is discouraging that the psychiatric community has seen fit to encourage the extroverted bias of our society" (Lane 2007, 78).

3. As we will see, this is also true in the history of our own Euro-American culture. Patricia McDaniel (2003), for instance, has shown how shyness was regarded as a virtuous character trait for women in medieval Europe. She goes on to show how early American colonists cultivated the Protestant disposition of meekness, modesty, and extreme humility and how these habits began to fade in the early twentieth century as advice manuals began promoting the values of individual self-expression, poise, and being charming as keys to success in a capitalist economy.

4. Complicating matters, there appears to be no corresponding disorder in the DSM that captures behavior on the opposite end of the spectrum, namely extroversion. Although Spitzer argued that extreme forms of extroversion were visible in manic disorder and chronic hypomanic disorder, the qualities of being outgoing, competitive, and assertive were certainly not pathologized; they were indicators of mental health (Lane 2007, 82). Indeed, successful treatment of social phobia usually involves the control and management of symptoms so that one can competently "pass" as someone with the socially preferable traits of extroversion (Scott 2005, 2006).

5. Hermeneutic psychiatry interprets these meanings in terms of prejudgments or "prejudices," a priori conditions that constitute our being, making it possible for things to matter to us in one way rather than another. As Gadamer writes: "It is not so much our judgments as our prejudices that constitute our being. . . . Prejudices are not necessarily unjustified or erroneous, so that they inevitably distort the truth. In fact, the historicity of our existence entails the prejudices [that], in the literal sense of the word, constitute the initial directedness of our whole ability to experience. Prejudices are biases of our openness to the world. They are simply conditions whereby we experience something" (1977, 9).

Chapter Seven

Situating Stress

Neurasthenia and Medically Unexplained Syndromes

In 1881, New York neurologist George M. Beard published *American Nervousness, Its Causes and Consequences: A Supplement to Nervous Exhaustion (Neurasthenia)*. In this expansive and meandering work, Beard explored the explosive growth of a new psychosomatic condition called "neurasthenia," in which mental distress emerged in the form of physical symptoms due to the deficiency or exhaustion of what he called "nerve force." He identified a vast number of symptoms, including: neuralgia, dyspepsia, hay fever, diabetes, sensitivity to narcotics and various drugs, depression, premature baldness, sensitivity to cold and heat, tooth decay, chronic catarrh, infertility, hysteria, inebriety, fatigue, and impotence (Beard 1881, vi-xi).[1] Beard attributed the rise of neurasthenia both to a hereditary predisposition and to the wrenching social upheavals of modernization at the end of the nineteenth century, as large swaths of the post–Civil War population migrated from slow-paced rural communities to chaotic and bustling cities in the Northeast and Midwest. With this movement, men abandoned their traditional vocations as manual tradesmen and farmers for new roles in office buildings, and women began to leave their stable domestic roles as wives and mothers to compete with men in universities and professional careers. Beard also cited the stressors emerging from the new technologies of industrialization such as the periodical press, the telegraph, telephone, and steam engine, as well as the ubiquity of mechanical clocks and watches that "compel us to be on time and excite the habit of looking to see the exact moment" (1881, 103).[2]

These factors, taken together, contributed to the excessive strain on mental health and helped explain Beard's claim that "the chief and primary cause [of neurasthenia]" is not the result of some organic pathology but of "modern

civilization [itself]" (1881, vi). By the turn of the century, neurasthenia had
spread to the other side of the Atlantic to Europe's urban centers.[3] Influential
cultural figures such as sociologist Max Weber and novelist Marcel Proust
received the diagnosis, and neurasthenic characters became increasingly
fashionable in the fiction of writers such as Edith Wharton, Theodore Dreis-
er, Henry James, and Thomas Mann. Indeed, the diagnosis became so common in the United States that William James referred to it as "Americanitis,"
and the massive drugstore chain Rexall Drugs produced a chloroform-laced
"Americanitis Elixir" for the "man of business, weakened by the strain of
[his] duties" (Osnos 2011).

Neurasthenia eventually fell out of favor in the United States[4] by the end
of the Great War due to its diagnostic vagueness, its unproven theory of
nervous energy, and the ambiguous breadth of its symptoms, but today we
are seeing the symptoms of neurasthenia emerge once again in the proliferation of functional somatic conditions such as fibromyalgia and chronic fatigue syndrome. These conditions are regarded as "syndromes" rather than
"diseases" because their medical etiology is unknown, and the conditions
cannot be confirmed through standard diagnostic procedures (Boulton 2018).
They are classified as syndromes solely on the basis of a wide grouping of
symptoms that look strikingly similar to Beard's neurasthenia. In what follows, we will explore the medicalization of neurasthenia and show how it
undermines the hermeneutic value of Beard's account by failing to engage
the socio-historical forces that contributed to its emergence. Rather than
viewing the neurasthenic from a reductive naturalistic perspective, as a discrete causally determined organism, Beard viewed the neurasthenic from the
perspective of being-in-the-world, as a situated existence already embedded
in the contextual upheavals of modernity. This situation not only shapes the
way we experience, feel, and perform our bodies; it also informs how we
interpret and give meaning to our mental stress and exhaustion. More importantly, it reveals why it is consoling to have this kind of suffering explained
in medical rather than psychiatric terms because it creates the impression that
the experience is medically legitimate or "real," even if the biomedical cause
remains elusive.

NEURASTHENIA AND NATURALISM: A BRIEF HISTORY

The diagnosis of neurasthenia emerged against the backdrop of enormous
successes in the natural sciences in the nineteenth century in areas such as
anatomy and physiology, zoology, evolutionary biology, and the emerging
field of neurology, of which Beard was a pioneer. These successes contributed to the loss of religious authority and an increasing fascination and faith
in the methods of natural science to discover and explain the truth about

human suffering. In the midst of these breakthroughs, as Heidegger writes, "it is as if science alone could provide objective truth. Science *is* the new religion" (ZS1, 18). This secular turn not only contributed to the emergent vocational prestige and cultural power of modern doctors, it also influenced the naturalistic paradigm that has fundamentally transformed the ways in which medical science interprets pathology.[5]

As we saw in chapter 1, naturalism in medicine entails both an epistemological and a metaphysical assumption. From an epistemological standpoint, it generally presupposes that the view of theoretical detachment and the objective procedures of empirical science are best suited to gain knowledge of the ailing body. From a metaphysical standpoint, it assumes a mechanistic position of physicalism, that all manifestations of illness are constituted in terms of physical substances in causal interaction and that these interactions can be quantified under mathematical laws. Thus naturalism, in Heidegger's words, "remains bound to the principle of causality, and thus [goes] along with the objectification of everything that is" (ZS1, 233). This paradigm creates the objectifying picture that characterizes modern medicine today, where an illness is considered "real" only insofar as there is some lesion, abnormality, or deviation from normal functioning that is visible via anatomical or physiological-chemical observation.

The result is a form of biological reductionism, where any pathology, if it is to be considered legitimate, must have a physical or biochemical origin. Thus, when it comes to the disordered thoughts and perceptions that characterize mental illness, the nineteenth-century Dutch physiologist Jakob Moleschott writes, "The brain secretes thoughts [in the same way] as the kidney secretes urine" (cited in Szasz 2007, 47). This brand of reductionism was evident in the way American medicine framed its understanding of nervous disorders at the turn of the century. Indeed, it could be argued that one of the reasons Beard's account of neurasthenia became a diagnostic juggernaut is because it was viewed as "a physical, not a mental state" (Beard 1881, 17). By 1900, neurasthenia had become the single most common diagnosis in the area of neuropathy and psychopathology (Shorter 1996). By tracing its origin to a congenital weakness of the nervous system, Beard's thesis made it real from the perspective of naturalism, and this gave it scientific legitimacy. Although many of its most pronounced symptoms were psychological—including crippling phobias, depression, panic anxiety, and compulsiveness—its status as a physical disease meant that the medical establishment could take sufferers seriously. It was not madness or moral failing that triggered the nervous breakdown, but a physiological depletion of the body's finite reserves of electrical "nerve force."

By removing the stigma of shame and fear associated with mental illness, neurasthenia was often viewed positively, not only as a mark of a highly evolved and refined nervous system but of a man's commitment to the Protestant values of industriousness and productivity or, in the case of women, of sensitivity and literary proclivities. Emerging in the busy urban corridors of the East Coast, it was initially viewed as the signature disorder of middle class "brain workers"—as opposed to rural "muscle workers"—whose drive and ambition could not match the frantic pace of a modern capitalist society. Physician George Drinka describes the phenomenon in terms of a person

> with a nervous tendency [who] is driven to think, to work, to strive for success. He presses himself and his life force to the limit, straining his circuits. Like an overloaded battery, or like Prometheus exhausted from reaching too high for the fire of the gods, the sufferer's electrical system crashes down, spewing sparks and symptoms and giving rise to neurasthenia. (1984, 191)

In this way, neurasthenia provided both a scientifically legitimate (i.e., naturalistic, physical) and culturally accepted (i.e., burnout, overwork) justification for being sick (Abbey & Garfinkel 1991). Rather than being viewed as insane, treated by a psychiatrist (or "alienist," as they were called at the time because they dealt with those who were alienated or estranged from society), and banished to the custodial care of the mental asylum, a prosperous neurasthenic could be cared for privately by a medical doctor, a neurologist trained in general pathology and internal medicine, and given the standard somatic treatment of the time: usually a combination of bed rest, a mild diet, electrical stimulation, hydrotherapy, and massage (Freedman 1987; Shorter 1997). This is how neurasthenia exploded in popularity at the turn of the century, becoming a catch-all diagnosis for anyone suffering from inchoate feelings of exhaustion, pain, anxiety, and nervousness. But almost as quickly as it emerged as a diagnostic behemoth, neurasthenia began to fade, eventually disappearing from American medicine altogether. This decline can be attributed to a number of overlapping factors.

First, what contributed to the staggering popularity of the diagnosis also contributed to its precipitous decline, namely the sheer broadness of its definition. Beard identified over seventy-five possible symptoms of neurasthenia, with the result that virtually anyone could be diagnosed with the condition. In terms of neurasthenia-related phobias alone, he listed: "fear of lightning, fear of responsibility, fear of open places, fear of closed places, fear of society, fear of being alone, fear of fears, fear of contamination, fear of everything" (Beard 1881, 7). As a result, "one found [neurasthenia] everywhere," as a French author wrote at the time, "in the salons, at the theater, in the novels, at the palace. By virtue of it, one explained the most disparate reactions of the individual: suicide and decadent art, adornment and adultery; it became the giant of neuropathy" (cited in Chatel & Peele 1970, 37). The ubiquity of neurasthenia's symptoms made the disorder virtually impossible to classify with any precision. In describing what he called "the caprice" of the condition, Beard acknowledged that "sufferers often times wonder and complain that they have so many symptoms [because] their pain and distress attack so many parts and organs" (Beard 1880, 76). This diagnostic ambiguity resulted in increasing skepticism in the medical community, eventually becoming "the garbage can of medicine" (Wessely 1990, 47).

The decline was also marked by the fact that neurasthenia's advocates could not identify a physiological cause. Beard's belief was that it was a physical disorder of weakened nerve cells characteristic of a hereditary or congenital condition. The stronger one's heredity, the more strain an individual could endure before succumbing to "nervous bankruptcy," and vice versa (Gossling 1987, 84–85). Beard thought that is was the dramatic social, economic, and technological changes taking place in America at the time that served as a trigger for those with a congenital weakness of nerve force. As he puts it:

> The force in [the] nervous system. . . is limited; and when new functions are interposed in the circuit, as modern civilization is constantly requiring us to do, there comes a period sooner or later, varying in different individuals, and at different times of life, when the amount of force is insufficient to keep all the lamps actively burning; those that are weakest go out entirely, or, as more frequently happens, burn faint and feebly—they do not expire, but give an insufficient and unstable light. (1881, 99)

The neurasthenic, in short, could not endure the mental strain of a country that was becoming rapidly Americanized. The problem, of course, is that Beard's thesis remained scientifically untestable. Yet, even though physicians could not identify an organic cause for neurasthenia, they could not deny that a condition existed that was overwhelming a large swath of metropolitan Americans, incapacitating individuals who were previously living successful and productive lives (Freedman 1987).[6] The question for physicians was whether or not it could be demonstrated that it was a single disease, or if a more precise nosology could identify specific disorders that existed within this broad classification. And it was the issue of nosology that sealed neurasthenia's fate in America.

NEURASTHENIA, PSYCHIATRY, AND THE CRISIS OF VALIDITY

In 1895, Freud published an influential paper entitled "On the grounds of detaching a particular syndrome from neurasthenia under the description of anxiety neurosis." This signaled one of the first attempts to provide a more rigorous system of classification, parceling out "anxiety neurosis" and "hysteria" from the broad category of neurasthenia. Shortly thereafter, Freud's contemporary, Pierre Janet, did the same with "compulsivity," detaching it from neurasthenia. These diagnostic changes meant far fewer were suffering from the condition (Gossling 1987; Wessely 1990). Although fin de siècle figures like Freud, Janet, and Jean-Martin Charcot were trained as neurologists and were committed to the idea of a physical origin to nervous disorders, they did not rely exclusively on the trademark somatic therapies of the day such as bed rest, electrical stimulation, massage, and water and thermal therapies. They focused instead on psychological processes or disorders of the mind, with the idea that the physical symptoms of neurosis might arise as the result of unconscious, usually libidinous, conflicts that emerged in early childhood. With this turn, psychotherapy (or the "talking cure") was born as a way of verbally accessing long-repressed sexual desires, traumas, and fantasies. Using dialogical techniques such as dream analysis, free association, and transference, the therapist would help the patient become aware of the their unconscious conflicts, and this awareness might free them of the physical symptoms of neurosis, demonstrating, in the words of one of Charcot's students, "that the body could be cured by the mind" (cited in Shorter 1997, 138).

Although the talking cure became wildly popular with middle- and upper-class society in twentieth-century America and was generally recognized by the medical establishment as offering useful therapeutic techniques to treat neurosis, its scientific foundations remained dubious. This is because psychoanalysis did not fit well into the empirical framework of naturalism. The assumption that an individual's neurotic affects and behavior could be explained, for example, in terms of repressed libidinous fantasies did not meet the standards of ocular evidence and testability that characterize empirical science. As opposed to somatic medicine, there is no way to physically locate, test for, or measure the source of repression or psychic conflict that manifests neurotic symptoms. Unlike physical abnormalities of blood, muscle, or bone, the abnormalities of the mind cannot be directly observed because, obviously, mental phenomena are not physical substances. The psychiatrist cannot point to a lesion or marker in the brain that secretes abnormal thoughts and affects. As a result, they can only infer that a given mental disorder or abnormality exists based on theoretical assumptions, that is, on the metapsychology of the therapist. But such inferences are unscientific precisely because they are impossible to empirically refute or falsify.

As we saw earlier, in the latter half of the twentieth century, with advances in neuroscience, pharmacology, and molecular genetics, psychiatry attempted to regain its footing in the natural sciences by embracing a more empirical and biologically informed approach to mental illness. Central to this shift was the rejection of the ideology and jargon of psychoanalysis in DSM-III, with the aim of implementing a system of disease classification based on empirically observable symptoms. This was done by eliminating the broad and ideologically loaded category of "neurosis" altogether and carving it up into more precise and reliable disease classifications. Having addressed the affective dimensions of neurasthenia by eliminating neurosis, the DSM taskforce also addressed its somatic symptoms. It did this by eradicating the archaic category of "hysteria" and replacing it with a new diagnostic label, "somatoform disorder." Regarded as a "conversion disorder," in which emotional or mental distress manifested in terms of physical symptoms, the diagnosis was meant to capture those patients who presented with symptoms like chronic pain, dizziness, weakness, gastrointestinal issues, and fatigue but had no demonstrable physical cause. For diagnostic precision, this category was also broken up into a number of discrete disorders.

But discarding the ideology of psychoanalysis and the antiquated categories of neurosis and hysteria did little to address the core issue of scientific validity. And sufferers of enigmatic nervous disorders today remain, as ever, haunted by the specter that what they experience is "imaginary," "unreal," or "in their heads." To this end, I want to suggest that the enduring skepticism about the validity of psychiatric diagnoses may shed light on the renewed interest in medically unexplained somatic syndromes such as fibromyalgia and chronic fatigue syndrome that bear a striking resemblance to neurasthenia. By emphasizing a medical or nonpsychiatric explanation of symptoms, the diagnosis creates the consoling impression of legitimacy even if there is no physical evidence to justify it. From a hermeneutic perspective, this is crucial for the narrative integrity and self-constitution of the sufferer.

HERMENEUTICS, SOMATIZATION, AND MEDICALLY UNEXPLAINED SYNDROMES

One of the advantages of approaching questions of health and illness from a hermeneutic perspective, as we have seen, is the way in which it reconfigures our conception of the self. Rather than viewing the self in naturalistic terms, as a causally determined physical substance, hermeneutic psychiatry sees it as an interpretive activity, where we exist in the narrative identities and self-interpretations that we project for ourselves. In this view, it is not *what* we are that is important but *how* we are, that is, how we ceaselessly fashion and refashion our own being as our lives unfold. What distinguishes us from animals, then, is the fact that we are "self-interpreting," that we create or understand who we are by interpreting and giving meaning to our physiological givenness (Taylor 1985). When we suffer from nervous exhaustion, diffuse pain, and anxiety, it is accordingly up to each of us to understand it, to imbue those symptoms with the intelligibility and significance that they have. Moreover, the meanings we give to our suffering are always embedded in a particular socio-historical context. Thus, the hermeneutic self is never regarded as encapsulated subject separate and distinct from the world. Rather, as Heidegger explains, "self and world belong together. [They] are not two beings like subject and object. . . . Self and world are the basic determination of [human existence] itself in the unity of the structure of being-in-the-world" (BP, 297).

As a relational way of being, our interpretations are limited or constrained by the meanings made available by our historical situation. The world opens up an array of possible ways for us to understand and make sense of our suffering, and because our interpretative context today is shaped so decisively by the paradigm of natural science, it is easy to see how the symptoms of neurasthenia are reborn in functional somatic syndromes like fibromyalgia and chronic fatigue syndrome.[7] This is why, as Robert Aronowitz cautions, "[there is] a market for somatic labels . . . in the large pool of 'stressed-out' or somaticizing patients who seek to disguise an emotional complaint or to 'upgrade' their diagnosis from a nebulous (i.e. psychiatric) one to a legitimate disease" (1991, 97).

This process can be described as "somatization," referring to a type of narrative construction where exhaustion, diffuse pain, and stress arising largely out of the situated upheavals and emergencies of living are experienced and explained as physical disorders, even in the absence of evidence (Lipowski 1988). Consider the case of Linda.

> Linda had spurned previous recommendations for psychiatric counseling. She would not accept that she might have a psychiatric illness, and was angry, rather than relieved, when doctors implied that "Nothing is wrong with you" and that "It is all in your head." She was convinced that something was physically wrong, and she wanted [the doctor] to identify and treat the problem. (Young 2003, 165)

Although physicians would usually treat Linda's condition as psychosomatic—as a somatic presentation of mental illness—for sufferers there is something deeply consoling when it is explained in physical terms. This is because it allows the patient to fashion a narrative that fits into the culturally accepted paradigm of naturalism. Even though functional somatic syndromes are medically dubious, the fact that they are regarded as physical rather mental illnesses is often sufficient for the patient to construct an account of suffering in a way that is not only intelligible but also culturally legitimate. The terms "fibromyalgia" and "chronic fatigue syndrome," then, are not just useful diagnostic labels. For patients, they are symbols that reflect a specific discursive context and help to create a meaningful identity. As physician Jerome Groopman (2000) explains, "Of all the words a doctor uses, the name he gives the illness has the greatest weight. . . . With a name, the patient can construct an explanation of his illness not only for others but for himself."

On the hermeneutic view, language is not a reference to lexical entities in the mind that designate or represent various states of affairs. Indeed, as Heidegger explains, language is not necessarily linguistic at all:

> Languages are not themselves extant like things. Language is not identical with the sum total of all the words printed in a dictionary; instead . . . *language is as Dasein is, because it exists, it is historical.* (BP, 208, my emphasis)

The suggestion here is that words, expressions, and gestures emerge and make sense only against a background of meanings opened by the shared practices of a historical people. This means the words used in diagnostic medicine are expressive of the meanings of a wider culture and are just as valuable as the physician's stethoscope, syringe, or scalpel because they allow the patient to fashion an intelligible self-interpretation. This helps to sharpen the distinction between the neurological aspects of "disease" and the lived-experience of "illness." If the physician's instruments treat and measure disease, it is their words that allow the patient to give meaning to their experience. Where the language of spirits, sin, and guilt was expressive of the context of meaning that allowed people to make sense of their suffering in the Middle Ages, for example, the language of biomedicine is expressive of our context today. This helps explain why, instead of going to a psychiatrist for complaints of inchoate feelings of pain and fatigue, insomnia, racing heart, digestive problems, or difficulty concentrating, we go to a medical specialist to validate our experience. We seek an immunologist to receive a diagnosis of chronic fatigue syndrome, a rheumatologist for a fibromyalgia diagnosis, a neurologist for tension headache, a cardiologist for atypical chest pain and palpitations, or a gastroenterologist for irritable bowel syndrome. By medicalizing these symptoms instead of situating them in their context, the patient feels validated, that there is a real medical cause to his or her suffering even if the physician does not see it this way (Barker 2005; Hearn 2009).

It is important to note, then, that those diagnosed with medically unexplained syndromes often have an accompanying psychiatric disorder, and the treatment is often the same as the treatment for anxiety and depressive disorders. Indeed, the only medications approved by the FDA to treat fibromyalgia—Lyrica, Cymbalta, and Savella—are antidepressants. Even so, patients generally favor a functional somatic diagnosis because it avoids the stigma of unreality often associated with mental illness (Wessely 1990). Receiving a medical diagnosis rather than a psychiatric one is important for the sufferer because it demonstrates legitimacy in the discursive context of biomedicine. And the ongoing hope underlying somatization is that it is only a matter of time before an actual cause can be found, an ocular confirmation of pathology through computerized axial tomography (CAT), for example, or functional magnetic resonance imaging (fMRI). And excitement builds in the medical community with the discovery of each new cause, whether it is measurable deficiencies in neurotransmitters like serotonin, low levels of somatotropin or growth hormone, or the poor sensory motor functioning of "substance P" (Groopman 2000). But in the meantime, the diagnosis of fibromyalgia or chronic fatigue syndrome presents its own problems for sufferers because, in the absence of evidence, they become, like Beard's neurasthenia over a century ago, "irritable everything syndromes," a trash bin of unexplained and unconfirmed symptoms (Barker 2005). As one fibromyalgia sufferer explains:

> You go online, and everything is a symptom of fibromyalgia. I was thinking the other day my hair is thinning and then I look online and it's a symptom. Everything is basically a symptom. Everything I get now, every little twinge, everything I'm just like, oh its fibromyalgia. And then I have to like really tell myself it might just be normal. Because I don't think all my symptoms are fibromyalgia. I don't think my headaches are, because I've had those for a long time. I don't think my sleep disturbances are, because I think that's just related to stress. So, it's easy when you've been given this word fibromyalgia to just put everything into it. . . . And that's why the boundaries between things have been sort of muddied, because everything could be fibromyalgia. But maybe hair loss is fibromyalgia. Maybe everything is fibromyalgia. (Boulton 2018, 6)

Thus, even though fibromyalgia and chronic fatigue syndrome carry the whiff of medical legitimacy, the legitimacy is an illusion. The sufferer still feels marginalized by the medical community because the diagnosis is in no way verifiable. As one woman writes, "I think that the word fibromyalgia seems to be completely *obsolete*. It just means, 'you're ill and we don't know what's wrong with you and we can't fix you,' that's all it means to me basically. I feel isolated with this diagnosis" (Boulton 2018, 7). Indeed, even if a biomedical fact were discovered, it is still up to the sufferer to understand and give meaning to their experience based on the interpretative resources opened up by their historical situation.

To this end, hermeneutic psychiatry dissolves the traditional bifurcation between "facts" and "values." From the standpoint of our situated existence, there are no brute, valueless facts. Reducing our experiences to physiological and biochemical causes is to deny the qualitative meaning and value we bring to them. Indeed, on closer view, the allegedly neutral and objective explanations of biochemistry are themselves value laden insofar as they emerge against the background of a common language and are viewed by Euro-American culture in qualitative terms as "valid" or "real." We can make sense of our experiences only through the language we grow into. Biomedical reductionism betrays this aspect of enculturation and the complexity and ambiguity of being-in-the-world, and this brings us back to the original value of Beard's account.

Although his theory of nerve force was scientifically unfounded, what makes Beard's account so relevant today is how it critically engages the meaning-structures of modernity itself. Instead of regarding the neurasthenic as a discrete object distinct from his or her relational context, Beard focused on the broad social and cultural upheavals taking place at the end of the nineteenth century, and he introduced the possibility that simply *existing* amidst these upheavals might be unhealthy.[8] By attending to the destabilizing social forces associated with turn-of-the-century American life—urbanization, industrialization, the insecurities of a market economy, new transportation and communication technologies, and the emergent dominance of clock-time—Beard recognized that neurasthenia was "an inevitable reaction to the excessive strain of mental and physical life" (1881, 83). As a physician, approaching questions of health and illness in a historically contextualized way, he saw the obvious, that the human being is not an atomistic body but an interpretative way of being that is already bound up in the world.

Today, in the face of corporate downsizing and the outsourcing of cheap labor to foreign markets, millions of Americans have been thrown into the precariat, a "gig economy" without job security, steady paychecks, health insurance, or retirement benefits. An advertisement from the lucrative ride-sharing company Uber speaks to those living precariat lives with the euphemism that everyone needs to "get their side hustle on." Of course, we need a side hustle today because we may be one paycheck away from being homeless or going bankrupt. The kind of chronic insecurity associated with neoliberal capitalism has fundamentally transformed our lives, exacerbating feelings of exhaustion and stress. Philosopher Carl Cederström documents how from 1973 to 2006 the American worker has added 180 hours to their annual working schedule, while wages have essentially remained flat. This trend has increasingly blurred the work-life balance, even colonizing our sleep habits. At the turn of the century, for example, the average American slept a full ten hours a night. Today, we sleep only six and a half hours, and even then, we often wake up in the middle of the night to check email (Cederström 2018, 96–97). Perpetually on alert and without even the basic protections of sleep to recalibrate our nervous systems, Beard's conclusion seems self-evident, that "nervous sensitiveness and nervous diseases ought to increase with the progress of modern civilization; and neurasthenia would naturally be more abundant in the present than in the last century" (1881, 137).

Beard's account of the toxic effects of an overstimulated, insecure, and mechanized existence not only reflects contemporary descriptions of American life as perpetually "overwhelmed," "stressed," and "burned out." It also opens the possibility for a deeper analysis of the particularities of nervous distress. This is especially interesting as it pertains to issues of gender. Whereas for men, neurasthenia was once widely regarded as a mark of ambition and drive, "[an] acceptable and even impressive illness . . . ideally suited to a capitalistic society and to the identification of masculinity with money and property" (Showalter 1985, 135), for women, the situation is far more complex. Among those suffering from neurasthenia at the turn of the century, women were disproportionately represented. And today, the vast majority of those complaining of medically unexplained somatic syndromes are women, including nearly 90 percent of all fibromyalgia sufferers (Barker 2005; Groopman 2000). Rather than attributing this overrepresentation to the idiosyncrasies of a woman's reproductive organs and hormones, Beard took a broad hermeneutic view, focusing on the changing social roles and meanings for women in the new industrialized economy, her entry and acceptance into colleges and the professions, and her emergent ambition and drive (Abbey & Garfinkel 1991).

Although criticized as a misogynist by regarding motherhood and domesticity as a woman's natural state,[9] Beard's view resonates with the concerns of contemporary feminist social critics by exposing the limits of medicalization and drawing our attention to the material forces that produce and reproduce our nervous distress. This not only helps frame what Betty Friedan in *The Feminine Mystique* (1963) called "the problem that has no name," referring to the social conformism of the post–World War II economy that pushed women into lives of empty domesticity, resulting in "housewife neurosis" and its accompanying symptoms of fatigue, pain, emotional irritability, and despair (Shuster 2011). It also situates the gendered incarnation of fibromyalgia and chronic fatigue syndrome today as women struggle with the precariat economy and rapidly changing social roles, busily trying to balance careers, family obligations, lower pay, and ongoing sexual harassment. In this way, Beard's work anticipates hermeneutic accounts of the relational complexity of being-in-the-world and creates an opening for health-care professionals to adopt a more nuanced and contextualized perspective when it comes to the experience and interpretation of nervous suffering. While it is true that medicalizing this kind of suffering as a somatic condition may create a consoling sense of legitimacy under the paradigm of naturalism, it fails to critically engage the historical context that made the paradigm possible in the first place. Hermeneutic psychiatry always begins from the standpoint of being-in-the-world, that we exist only in the meanings that we create for ourselves, and that it is only through these shared self-interpretations that we can experience and make sense of our suffering.

In the final chapter, we expand our discussion of the psychopathologies of modernity, focusing now on the explosion of a new rage condition in America, referred to in the DSM as "intermittent explosive disorder." Rather than viewing this disorder in terms of a set of symptoms that resides inside the individual, we again take a hermeneutic view, examining the meaning-structures of American life that may be contributing to our collective rage. I suggest that the condition may have something to do with the way we, as Americans, tend to interpret ourselves as radically free individuals. Viewing ourselves in this atomistic way means there are no defining relations to anything outside ourselves, creating a situation that is stripped of any sense of belongingness or moral orientation besides our own personal preferences and desires. The result is a uniquely American vision of authenticity, where we are "true to ourselves" only to the extent that we pursue our own wants and are free from any externally imposed authority or constraints. But this ideology of individualism and unmoored freedom may also manifest feelings of impotence, loneliness, and moral confusion. Without a framework of human connections and shared meanings to guide us, we have no idea of what to do or how to act, which suggests that the ubiquitous explosions of violence and rage in America may have something to do with the historical meanings that shape our current self-understanding. And these meanings may be concealing or covering over an older sense of authenticity, where we understand ourselves not as masterful subjects but as relational beings who are fundamentally vulnerable and mutually dependent on each other.

NOTES

1. The ideas in *American Nervousness* emerged out of an earlier article of Beard's (1869) entitled "Neurasthenia or nervous exhaustion."

2. German sociologist Georg Simmel develops this idea in his pioneering 1903 essay, "The Metropolis and Mental Life," by exploring the psychic costs of clock-time, where "punctuality, calculability, [and] exactness are forced upon life by . . . metropolitan existence" (1997, 177).

3. It is interesting to note that neurasthenia eventually stretched across class and gender lines in a way that was unique among functional somatic conditions. It was diagnosed first among upper-middle-class women, then among "stressed out" middle-class businessmen, and finally among the lower working classes before vanishing altogether from American medicine (Gosling 1987; Wessely 1990).

4. Although it eventually disappeared as a diagnostic entity in the United States, the diagnosis continues to be applied in Europe, is still listed in the latest edition of the *International Classification of Diseases* (ICD-10), and is used widely in countries such as Japan, Korea, China, Australia, and Russia.

5. This historical shift is evident in, for example, the ways in that various forms of social deviance earlier regarded as religious or moral failings by priests—such as alcoholism, depression, and homosexuality—came to be medicalized by doctors in the twentieth century (Aho and Aho 2008, 65–70).

6. Beard's theory was further undermined by the discovery of hormones in 1902, which convinced physicians that they had identified a specific causal agent—a chemical or hormonal imbalance that fit nicely into the mechanistic paradigm of naturalism. The problem with this early version of the chemical imbalance theory was that, although hormones certainly exist, it could not be demonstrated that they in fact caused nervous disorders (Chatel & Peele 1970).

7. In listing the symptoms of neurasthenia, Beard refers to "profound exhaustion," "pains in the back," and "heaviness in the loins and limbs," which today could indicate a diagnosis of chronic fatigue syndrome. He cited "localized peripheral numbness and hyperesthesia," "ticklishness," "local spasms of muscles," and "vague pains and flying neuralgias," which fit the

diagnostic profile of fibromyalgia. And he cited special idiosyncrasies with regard to "food," "cramps," "nervous dyspepsia," and "indigestion" (1881, 7–8), which resemble the symptoms of irritable bowel syndrome.

8. To this end, Beard anticipates the reflections of Medard Boss, who claims "the vast majority of all modern ailments already belong to the illnesses of man which are called by the unfortunate term 'psychosomatic.' They all finally have their origin in the sick person's comportment to the modern industrial society of our time, with which he could not cope in a way worthy of a human being" (ZS1, 297).

9. Beard and his contemporary, neurologist S. Weir Mitchell, warned against the educational, creative, and intellectual pursuits of women, as they contribute to her nervous exhaustion. After prescribing his notorious "rest cure" for writer and activist Charlotte Perkins Gilman, for instance, Mitchell implored her going forward to "live as domestic a life as possible. Have your child with you all the time. . . . Lie down an hour after each meal. Have but two hours' intellectual life a day. *And never touch pen, brush or pencil as long as you live*" (Gilman 1975, 96, my emphasis.).

Chapter Eight

Situating Rage

Alienation, Individualism, and American Authenticity

Recent polls suggest that the majority of Americans are angry at virtually everything (Duhigg 2019; Barford 2016). We are angry at the state of the economy for favoring the wealthy and failing to deliver well-paying jobs to middle-class Americans; at our immigration policy for the "browning" of America and the inability to secure the southern border; at Washington for its legislative gridlock, cronyism, and corruption; at our diminished standing in the world for failing to provide basic necessities like health care and an unwillingness to engage the global threat of climate change. Women are raging with the #MeToo movement after decades of suffering from sexual harassment and violence from men. Blacks are raging with #BlackLivesMatter in the wake of countless episodes of police brutality and the mass incarceration of their people. The national tinderbox is on full display on the nightly news as we witness explosions of road rage, airport rage, parking lot rage, office rage, and shopping rage. This, coupled with a grotesque escalation in mass shootings, is certainly telling us something about the stresses and frustrations of American life and is perhaps disclosing a new cultural mood. Indeed, it looks as if the post-war "age of anxiety" has been replaced by the "age of rage." A recent study funded by the National Institute of Mental Health (NIMH) found that up to 8.9 percent of adults, or roughly twenty-two million Americans, now struggle with impulsive rage issues and, according to the DSM, could be diagnosed with the psychiatric condition "intermittent explosive disorder" (Ingraham 2015).

Although intermittent explosive disorder didn't appear in the diagnostic lexicon until 1980, a version of the condition could be found in earlier editions of the DSM. In DSM-I, under the category of "passive-aggressive personality," it was defined as "a persistent reaction to frustration with irritability, temper tantrums, and destructive behavior" (APA 1952, 37). In DSM-II, it was identified as a stand-alone personality disorder called "explosive personality (Epileptoid personality disorder)" and characterized by "gross outbursts of rage or of verbal and physical aggressiveness" (APA 1968, 42–43). When DSM-III introduced intermittent explosive disorder for the first time, it was defined in terms of "several discrete episodes of loss of control and aggressive impulses resulting in serious assault or destruction of property [and] behavior that is grossly out of proportion to any precipitating psychosocial stressor" (APA 1980, 297). But with the publication of DSM-V, the phenomenon of diagnostic bracket creep begins to emerge. The criterion now claims that a diagnosis of the illness is warranted if there are recurrent outbursts of "[either] verbal aggression (e.g., temper tantrums, tirades, verbal arguments, or fights) *or* physical aggression toward property, animals or other individuals, occurring twice weekly, on average for a period of 3 months" (APA 2013, 466). By broadening the criterion with the claim that *either* verbal *or* physical aggression counts and eliminating the language of "serious assault and destruction of property," it appears that almost anyone could be suffering from the disorder (Hickley 2015). Someone who frequently yells at the television while watching the news; who erupts with temper tantrums after his football team loses; or who rages at other motorists while stuck in slow-moving traffic could conceivably receive the diagnosis. As psychologist Philip Hickley (2018) writes, "Prior to DSM-5, he wasn't mentally ill; he was just rude and vituperative." It is no surprise then that the NIMH found that nearly one in ten Americans could be diagnosed with the illness in their lifetime. Given the loose and expansive criterion in the DSM, it seems the number could easily be much higher. And the medicalization of rage, of course, doesn't end there. Due to the dominance of the medical model, the first line of defense in treating the disorder is almost always going to be medications, especially antidepressants, antianxiety agents, and mood stabilizers (such as lithium and anticonvulsants).

From the perspective of hermeneutic psychiatry, this kind of reductive and decontextualized account of American rage not only fails to scientifically "explain" (*erklären*) the phenomenon, as there is no direct evidence of a medical condition. More importantly, it does not attempt to "understand" (*verstehen*) the experience, that is, to situate it within the webs of meaning that are already shaping our affective lives and informing our self-interpretations. In developing a contextually robust understanding of rage, then, we have to approach the experience hermeneutically, from within the meaning-structures of modernity itself. To this end, it is helpful to bring Heidegger's account of being-in-the-world into conversation with the works of Dostoevsky, not because his major characters are so often filled with uncontrolled rage but because they are always historically situated, embedded in wrenching social upheavals as Russia endured a period of rapid modernization in the mid- to late nineteenth century. Of all his tortured characters, perhaps none embodies the conflicts of modernity (or is more rage-filled) than the "underground man," the unnamed voice behind Dostoevsky's famous novella, *Notes from the Underground* (1864). Here, in the oft-overlooked prologue to the story, Dostoevsky reveals his hermeneutic leanings, providing some insight into our own American situation, reminding the reader that it is precisely because of the disruptions of modernity that "such a man *must* exist in our society, when we consider the circumstances in the midst of which our society is formed" (2009, 1).

NIHILISM AND HOMELESSNESS

Heidegger's connection to Dostoevsky is well known (cf. Gerigk 2017). Dostoevsky is one of the few non-German figures that he consistently cites as an influence on *Being and Time*, and he kept a portrait of the Russian prominently displayed in his office. Indeed, after taking over Husserl's chair at the University of Freiburg, Heidegger personally oversaw the university library purchasing the complete works of Dostoevsky (Schmid 2011). But his most revealing references come in letters to his wife, Elfride. In one, written from the battlefields of Lorraine in 1918, Heidegger asks for two items to give him some comfort, a wedding-day photograph of Elfride "standing by the sunflower in [her] Worpswede dress [and a] copy of *The Brothers Karamazov*" (LW, 48, my emphasis). And in a revealing note from 1920, he tells Elfride that is was through the writings of Dostoevsky that he learned with it meant to have a "homeland" (*Heimat*) and to have one's "roots in the soil." He goes on to encourage her to read Dostoevsky's political writings in order to properly understand his own critique of modernity (LW, 72–73). But what does it mean to have one's roots in the soil, and how might the modern experience of uprootedness contribute to our explosions of rage?

The experience of being uprooted and homeless for both Dostoevsky and Heidegger is informed by the nihilistic mood that was washing over Europe and Russia in the mid- to late nineteenth century. Nietzsche famously refers to the predicament in terms of the "death of God," describing nihilism as the historical moment when "the highest values devaluate themselves. The aim is lacking; 'why?' finds no answer" (1968, 2). Without a shared conception of the sacred, there are no binding values or moral absolutes that we can turn to for guidance and inspiration. In Nietzsche's words,

> We have left the land behind and boarded the ship! We have burned our bridges—more than that, we have demolished the land behind us! Now, little ship, watch out! . . . The hours are coming when you will recognize that it is infinite, and that there is nothing more terrifying than infinity. *Alas, when*

homesickness for the land comes over you . . . there is no longer any "land."
(2001, 141, my emphasis)

Amongst the intelligentsia in Russia, this fin de siècle nihilism was largely viewed as a sign of progress, where secular reason, empirical science, and the laws of physics freed the Russian people from superstition and the authority of religious dogma. But for Dostoevsky, these newly imported values created an atmosphere of alienation and confusion. Indeed, all of Dostoevsky's mature (post-Siberian) works can be viewed as attacks on the younger generation of social reformers who were coming of age in the 1860s. He saw them as nihilists for rejecting the traditional values of the Eastern Church, for embracing rational egoism, and attempting to re-engineer society on the basis calculative principles like utilitarianism and scientific determinism. By embracing these secular ideals, Dostoevsky saw a historical people being cut away from their indigenous roots, resulting in explosions of madness, violence, and rage.

Dostoevsky's major characters are often incarnations of this conflict as they confront the ideology of the modern age.[1] Without the authority of the Eastern Church to guide them, they are uprooted and lost, free to construct whatever morality they want. In *Crime and Punishment* (1866), for example, Raskolnikov overhears a conversation in a bar and uses it to come up with his own theory to justify his murder of Alyona.

> Kill here, take her money, dedicate it to serving mankind, to the general welfare. Well—what do you think—isn't this petty little crime effaced by thousands of good deeds? For one life, thousands of lives saved from ruin and collapse. One death and a hundred lives—there's arithmetic for you? (1968, 73)

But Raskolnikov's selfishness and cold utilitarian calculus collide with the Christian values of self-sacrifice and brotherly love that he was raised with from childhood. He is torn apart by conflicting personalities, described as a man who is at once "magnanimous and kind . . . [but also] inhumanly cold and unfeeling to the point of inhumanity, as though he had two contradictory characters that keep changing places." (1968, 215)

Similarly, when Ivan Karamazov in *The Brothers Karamazov* (1880) learns that his half-brother committed suicide, he is driven insane by a sense of religious guilt that clashes with his own rational and atheistic worldview. "Conscience!" he tries to convince himself, "What is conscience? I make it up for myself. Why am I tormented by it? From the universal habit of mankind for seven thousand years. So let us give it up, and we shall be gods" (1957, 592). Dostoevsky describes Ivan's feelings of guilt as affective proof of God's presence, a presence that challenges Ivan to let go of his commitments to egoism and logic, to either accept the mystery of God or be destroyed by it. Dostoevsky writes:

> God, in whom Ivan disbelieved, and His truth were gaining mastery over his heart, which still refused to submit. "He'll either rise up in the light of truth, or . . . he'll perish in hate, revenging on himself and on everyone his having served a cause he does not believe in." (1957, 594)

Although he is presented as being newly modernized or "Europeanized," Ivan's guilt as well as his concerns for ultimate questions regarding human suffering and the meaning of life illuminate a repressed longing for the supernatural and the sacred traditions of the Russian people (Paris 2008, 184).

Characters like Raskolnikov, Ivan Karamazov, and the underground man can be read as expressions of Dostoevsky's conviction that Europe was in decline. It was losing touch with an older sense of spiritual community and self-sacrifice for the modern values of individualism, scientific progress, and crass materialism. Through the confusion and rage embodied in these characters, he offers a powerful critique of modernity, its uprootedness from the authority of tradition, and its conception of the self as atomistic and masterful. For Dostoevsky, this modern brand of individualism creates a deep sense of loneliness and disconnection, representing a kind of cultural sickness or depravity. Father Zossima, speaking for Dostoevsky in *The Brothers Karamazov*, explains:

> All mankind in our age is split up into units. Man keeps apart, each in his own groove; each one holds aloof, hides himself and hides what he has, from the rest. He ends up being repelled by others and repelling them. . . . For he is accustomed to rely upon himself alone and to cut himself off from the whole, he has trained himself not to believe in the help of others, in men and in humanity, and only trembles for fear he should lose his money and the privileges he has won from himself. Everywhere in these days men have ceased to understand that the true security is to be found in social solidarity rather than in isolated individual effort. But this terrible individualism must inevitably have an end, and all will suddenly understand how unnaturally they are separated from one another. (1957, 279)

Dostoevsky's critique of "terrible individualism" constitutes a decisive break with the modern existentialist tradition with which he is so often associated. One of the central themes of existentialism is the idea that the aim in life is to be authentic, that is, to be true to oneself as an individual in the face of nihilism. But the authentic self for Dostoevsky is not a voluntaristic subject who, freed from the stifling confines of tradition, heroically chooses his or her own values in the vacuum of God's death. If authenticity has something to do with self-realization, Dostoevsky shows that this can happen only in relation to others and the enduring values of a historical people, values that provide a deep sense of what matters in life. It is, as Charles Guignon writes, "an experience of the harmony of 'togetherness' or 'belongingness' expressed in the Russian word *sobornost*" (1993b, xli). On this account, the existentialist view of the self as radially free does not address the modern experience of homelessness and our propensities for rage; it only exacerbates it.

In this regard, Dostoevsky's writings reflect Heidegger's own critique of the "groundlessness" (*Bodenlosigkeit*) of modernity and the need to recover a "heritage" (*Erbe*) that has been covered over by the banal fads and fashions of modern life. This means, to the extent that we are absorbed in the latest tends, we are closed off from older sources of value that can give our lives a sense of shared direction and purpose. That modern life distorts and covers over our heritage in this way points to the importance of anxiety in Heidegger's early project, because it has the power to shake us out of everydayness and bring us face to face with who we are as finite, historically situated beings. In this sense, anxiety places me before my own temporal constitution as a "thrown project" (*geworfen Entwurf*). On the one hand, it discloses the fact that I am not a stable, self-subsisting thing but a "not yet," an unfinished way of being that, until death, is always pressing forward (or "projecting") into future possibilities. On the other hand, it discloses the fact that I am already thrown into a past, into a socio-historical situation that opens up meaningful possibilities that I can take over as my life unfolds. This is why Heidegger says, "Dasein 'is' its past in the way of its own Being" (BT, 20). It is this latter point that reveals Heidegger's commitment to the idea of *Heimat* and belongingness and his own break with the existentialist tradition. Temporally, my existence does not just stretch forward into possibilities that are not yet. It also stretches backward toward my "birth," toward my shared historical beginning.

The fact that I am thrown in this way means that the values and self-interpretations I choose are not ones that I alone create as a masterful subject. They are appropriated by the past that has been laid out before me, and they matter to me because they matter to the historical community to which I belong. In this sense, Heidegger, like Dostoevsky, rejects the existentialist idea that it is up to the individual alone to create his or her own values. Although we invariably lose sight of it in the surface dealings of everyday life, we are nonetheless already guided by a set of common values and a shared sense of right and wrong that belongs to our heritage. For Dostoevsky, this sense of being already guided by the past informs much of the confusion and rage of his major characters as the older values of community and self-sacrifice collide with the modern ideals of individualism, selfishness, and hedonism. When Dostoevsky speaks of the need of Russians "to return to their 'native soil,' to the bosom, so to speak, of their mother earth" (1957,

632), he is referring to the indigenous values of the Eastern Church. And this helps us get clear about what Heidegger means when, in *Being and Time*, he introduces the possibility of an authentic "retrieval" or "repetition" (*Wiederholung*) of the historical meanings of the past. He is referring to the shared autochthonous values that flow through the history of the West.

AMERICAN RAGE AND THE CULT OF AUTHENTICITY

In America today, we generally see ourselves as masterful, self-determined subjects. And we are authentic or true to ourselves insofar as we pursue our own desires and are free from external constraints. But for Dostoevsky, a life based on the relentless pursuit of freedom, pleasure, and self-affirmation is a sucker's game. It is not an expression of self-actualization but of bondage and self-destruction. To this end, he writes:

> The world has proclaimed the reign of freedom, especially of late, but what do we see in this freedom? Nothing but slavery and self-destruction! . . . Interpreting freedom as the multiplication and rapid satisfaction of desires, men distort their own natures, for many senseless and foolish habits and ridiculous beliefs are thus fostered. . . . [How] can a man shake off his habits, what can become of him if he is in such bondage to the habit of satisfying the innumerable desires he has created for himself. (Dostoevsky 1957, 289)

For Dostoevsky, genuine freedom has nothing to do with the willful satisfaction of our own desires. Such a view is inevitably self-defeating, placing us on the hedonic treadmill, where each time we satisfy a pleasure, it is followed by a feeling of emptiness, which results in a new craving for pleasure, creating an endless cycle of pleasures followed by feelings of emptiness followed by more attempts to feel pleasure (Guignon 1993b). According to Dostoevsky, we are truly free only when we are liberated from the bondage of our own narcissism and selfishness. Thus, when he claims our self-affirmation "distorts [our] true nature," he is suggesting that modern individualism is itself the problem.

But the idea of authenticity embodied in the voluntaristic subject appears to have a stranglehold on American identity. This ethos is a natural byproduct of what we described earlier as the culture of "personality" that emerged in early twentieth-century America with its emphasis on slick confidence, individuality, and salesmanship, eclipsing the older culture of "character" and its commitment to principles of humility, self-effacement, and religious duty. The culture of personality only grew stronger after World War II, as young bohemians and hippies rebelled against the boring conformism of their parents and human potential movements exploded on the scene, drawing on an eclectic mix of technologies—from psychedelic drugs and Gestalt and

Reichian psychotherapy, to shamanism and Eastern mysticism—to help us become individuals, to free ourselves in order to unlock and actualize our innermost desires. To this end, American youth were following Sartre's existentialist battle cry: "We want freedom for freedom's sake and in every particular instance" (2001, 306). Tuned in to the *Zeitgeist*, novelist Norman Mailer described this exhilarating reconfiguration of American identity in existentialist terms, as "the courage to be an individual," where we "divorce from society, exist without roots, [and] set out on that uncharted journey into the rebellious imperatives of the self" (cited in Cederström 2018, 47). But it is this call to freedom for Dostoevsky and Heidegger that perpetuates the modern experience of isolation and forlornness. Because in their view, there is no secure ground to stand on, no right way to act independent of our own individual wants and needs, and we are in no way bound to or dependent on others. If we are truly committed to the principle of what Robert Bellah (1985) referred to as "ontological individualism," of seeing the self as a discrete subject, a self-contained "I" with no defining relations to anything outside of ourselves, then there is no justification for our decisions other than our own subjective preferences.

In *The Culture of Narcissism* (1978), historian Christopher Lasch famously critiques this American brand of authenticity, in which the only thing that should guide our lives is freedom and the spontaneity of our individual desires, however transient and fleeting. Like Nike's iconic slogan "Just Do It" or the bumper sticker mantra "YOLO" ("You only live once"), the aim of the authentic individual is to "live for the moment . . . [to] live for oneself, not one's predecessors or [for] posterity" (Lasch 1978, 5). Lasch explores how this attitude of unguided freedom and narcissism is ultimately unfulfilling and identifies a number of overlapping characteristics that manifest in this kind of individual, including: "a sense of inner emptiness," "an intense fear of old age and death," "a fascination with celebrity," "deteriorating social relations," and most interesting, for our purposes, "*a boundless repressed rage*" (1978, 33, my emphasis). Existential psychotherapist Rollo May anticipated Lasch's cultural diagnosis, describing rage as a natural consequence of our own social displacement and lack of human connection. It is "the ultimate destructive substitute which surges in to fill the vacuum where there is no related-ness. . . . When inward life dries up, when feeling decreases and apathy increases, when one cannot affect or even genuinely *touch* another person, violence flares up as a daimonic necessity for contact, a mad drive forcing touch in the most direct way possible" (May 1969, 30–31). What this reveals is that the moral calling to be an individual in America, to rebel against authority and the stifling constraints of tradition all in an effort to connect with one's innermost self, is a sham. The cultural embrace of ontological individualism has created feelings of impotence, isolation, and moral confusion. Without a framework of common values to guide us, we have no idea of what to do and how to live. And this is precisely what enrages Dostoevsky's underground man. "We don't even know what *living* means now," he cries. "What it is, and what it is called! . . . We do not know what to join, what to cling to, what to love and what to hate" (Dostoevsky 2009, 96). On this reading, the explosions of violence and rage in America can be viewed as a reflection of our relentless pursuit of freedom and authenticity.

Carl Cederström (2018) explores this phenomenon by showing how the cult of authenticity born in the human potential movements of the 1960s and '70s has been colonized by neoliberal capitalism, creating a situation where selfishness and narcissism are not simply moral values; they are compulsory necessities for survival in an economy built on insecurity, ruthless competition, and self-promotion. The closing scene of the television series *Mad Men* captures an early manifestation of this phenomenon as advertising executive Don Draper sits with eyes closed in lotus position at the Esalen Institute on the California coast in 1970. Meditating with other searchers, a wry smile emerges on his face as he envisions a way to exploit the whole hippie scene for profit. And the iconic Coca Cola ad begins with images of men and women from the counterculture, bright and happy, authentically bound together by a single cause, singing the jingle, "I'd like to buy the world a Coke." Cederström describes how many of today's most successful corporations are adopting the same antiauthoritarian language of freedom and self-actualization to appeal to their workers, identifying how managers at corporations such as Levi Strauss & Co. are now referred to as "coaches," "facilitators," and "role models" whose aim is to help their employees "realize their full potential." The yoga apparel company lululemon has banned the word "meeting" from its corporate lexicon because of its authoritarian undertones, replacing it with the word "connect," where the goal of each connect is to "surprise and delight." The popular shoe-selling company Zappos openly encourages hedonism and self-expression of its employees with a website claiming: "We encourage you to be yourself and have fun. We don't promote work/life balance in the traditional sense, rather we believe in 'work/life integration.' We like having a good time at work, not just outside of it. . . . In a way, you might be taking a 'break from life' by working here!" (Cederström 2018, 84-88). By recasting the gray drudgery of the traditional nine-to-five workday, today's corporations have coopted the ideology of authenticity, promoting a kind of compulsory happiness with the bizarre assumption that one can be free and true to oneself by selling soft drinks, jeans, yoga pants, and shoes.

But, as Cederström reveals, something far more sinister is at play in corporate America. By embracing the rhetoric of individualism and self-actualization and blurring the line between life and work, today's corporations have actually created an environment of ceaseless labor, where it is not enough just to do your job, you also have to be passionate, happy, and fulfilled while you do it. And for corporations, the cult of authenticity's inward turn, its narrow focus on individual freedom and subjective pleasure, and its disregard for our dependency on others, creates an important diversion, turning our attention away from the broader political and economic injustices and inequities that neoliberal capitalism manifests. So while we continue to aggressively market and brand ourselves as optimistic, creative, and self-assured, we work ourselves to the bone and simmer with rage, repeating the empty maxim: "Be real, enjoy yourself, be productive—and most important, don't rely on other people to achieve these goals, because your fate is, of course, in your own hands" (Cederström 2018, 7).

In his book *The Burnout Society* (2015), philosopher Byung-Chul Han explores the psychic consequences of this social transformation, referring to ours as an "achievement society" (*Leistungsgesellschaft*), where each individual is pressured to be an entrepreneur of him or herself, resulting in a condition where "excess work and performance escalate into auto-exploitation" (2015, 11). We have moved beyond a situation where managers and supervisors are needed to discipline and regulate our behavior at the workplace. In the age of ontological individualism, the human being becomes "the *animal laborans* that exploits itself—and it does so voluntarily, without external constraints." (2015, 10) The result, for Byung-Chul, is a kind of neurological burnout, where

> the exhausted, depressive achievement-subject grinds itself down, so to speak. It is tired, exhausted by itself, and at war with itself. Entirely incapable of relying . . . on the Other, on the world, it locks jaws on itself; paradoxically, this leads the self to hollow and empty out. It wears out in a rat race run against itself. (2015, 42)

But, as Dostoevsky reminds us, it is the atomization of society and our collective inability to see ourselves as relational beings that is contributing to our current malaise. In his view, we have never been masterful individuals, and our fate has never been in our own hands. Indeed, it is the moral orientation of egoism, individual achievement, and self-reliance that makes us sick. This is why the underground man is such a tragic figure. He wants to see himself as radically free, but his unmoored freedom leaves him angry, confused, and lonely, triggering his delusional behavior, bizarre revenge fantasies, and impulsive need to hurt others. For Dostoevsky, the reason for the underground man's condition is simple; he has been "uprooted from the soil and has lost contact with the people" (2009, 11). And we see extreme incarnations of moral nihilism and rage in contemporary versions of the American antihero, in the unnamed narrator from Chuck Palahniuk's *Fight Club* (1999), for example, or Patrick Bateman in Bret Easton Ellis's *American*

Psycho (1991). Trapped in a cycle of empty hedonism, Ellis describes Bateman as someone who has lost his capacity for empathy and human connection to such an extent that he undergoes a kind of numbing depersonalization, where "there is *no real* me, only an entity, something illusory. . . . I simply am not there" (Ellis 1991, 367–77). And it is only through explosive acts of violence that he can be pulled out of this deadened state (cf. Aho 2016).

We see, then, that psychiatry's tendency to interpret rage as a discrete medical condition located inside the individual misses the mark. From a hermeneutic perspective, to understand American rage we must attend not merely to the symptoms but to one's "situatedness" (*Befindlichkeit*) as a whole. In this view, the mood of rage is already part of the collective atmosphere of our hyperindividualistic society. In Heidegger's words, "[it] assails us. It comes neither from 'outside' nor from 'inside': but arises out of being-in-the-world [itself]" (FCM, 176, my emphasis). It is because we have been habituated into an exhausting, lonely, and relentlessly competitive world that we are enraged in this way in the first place. Central to the therapeutic process of self-understanding, then, is recognizing the ways in which the meaning-structures of our historical situation are always working beyond our backs, constituting the mooded atmosphere into which we are thrown. The primary aim of hermeneutic psychiatry is not to defuse or eradicate rage with medication or cognitive and behavioral techniques but to provide a framework of meanings that allows the sufferer to understand his or her rage, to constructively express it, and come to grips with its sources. And this self-understanding can help broaden our conception of authenticity, allowing us to see that it does not have to be grounded in the modern ideologies of individualism and unconditional freedom, and that there are other ways to morally orient ourselves within the context of our own history.

But the idea, forwarded by Dostoevsky and Heidegger, that the cure for what ails us involves the recovery of a mythic past rooted in the indigenous values of a historical people, is deeply problematic, particularly in light of the conservative politics and anti-Semitism linked to both of them. Here, the "Jew" is accused once again of being the agent of cosmopolitanism and rootlessness. And the solution is to embrace Heideggerian rhetoric of *Blut und Boden, das Volk*, and *Heimat*. This is the implicit message of Donald Trump's "Make America Great Again" campaign, of Germany's *Alternative für Deutschland* movement, of Austria's *Identitären*, and of the antiliberal speeches of the Russian ideologue Alexander Dugin (Trawny 2018, 69; Dugin 2017). Yet, there is an aspect of historical retrieval in Heidegger's thought that may allow us to bypass this fraught political terrain and unsettle the more toxic assumptions of modern individualism. When Heidegger refers to "authentic historicality" (*eigentlichen Geschichtlichkeit*) in *Being and Time*, he is referring to a sense of belongingness to a heritage that places moral demands on us. As such, it illuminates the fact that we are not isolated subjects invariably motivated by pleasure and self-interest but beings that are mutually dependent on each other and bound together by shared values that can provide a sense of moral orientation for our lives.

Charles Guignon, well known for pioneering this interpretation of Heidegger, argues that our moral perspective is always rooted in the "stories and interpretations passed down in our historical community" (1993a, 287). When we see someone acting in overtly manipulative or selfish ways, for example, we usually respond spontaneously with a sense of disappointment because this kind of behavior conflicts with the values that emanate from the stories and interpretations of our Greek and Judeo-Christian forbearers, values we tacitly absorb in our everyday lives. As opposed to inauthentic Dasein who has forgotten its own heritage and simply drifts along with the fads and fashion of *das Man*, Guignon suggests authentic Dasein, shaken out of its tranquilized drift by anxiety, is awakened to deeper possibilities for living, possibilities that flow out of a shared historical source. This allows us to rethink Heidegger's controversial notions of a Dasein that "chooses his hero" (*seinen Helden wählt*) and retrieves his "fateful destiny" (*schicksalhaftes Geschick*). Although these ideas reflect the jargon of Nazism and certainly echo some of the darker themes in Heidegger's *Black Notebooks* (*Schwarze Hefte*) and his infamous Rectoral Address in 1933, Guignon puts forth the possibility that there may be something less sinister afoot. His interpretation illustrates how being authentic may have little to do with the isolated individual who soberly faces death and freely creates his or her own values in the absence of God. It is true, for Heidegger, that authenticity involves a decisive and clear-sighted recognition of our own finitude, but it also involves an awareness of our enmeshment in a shared heritage, a past that provides us with a value-rich context of archetypal figures, myths, and stories that can help us understand what it means to be human.

Flowing out of a common wellspring in the West, these stories have therapeutic power by showing how we can free ourselves from the cult of individualism and be opened up to an awareness of our "co-Dasein," that is, our mutual dependency and rootedness in the shared values of a historical people. This awareness not only serves as a powerful corrective to the forlornness, rage, and egoism that torment characters like Raskolnikov, Ivan Karamazov, and the underground man. It also concretizes Heidegger's idea of "choosing a hero." We can certainly choose, as Dostoevsky suggests we do, to model our lives after the image of Christ, where "we are all responsible to all and for all" (Dostoevsky 1957, 295). But Guignon shows that there are any number of cultural heroes, both secular and religious, whose stories can be "retrieved" and "repeated" to teach us the values of self-sacrifice, humility, and dependency on others. These stories, taken together, constitute a skein of meanings that we can draw on to create our own morally cohesive and structured life-story. Guignon's point is that "narrativizing" or "storyizing" our lives in this way continually brings with it a moral dimension because the resolution of the story usually entails "the achievement of some good taken as normative of our historical culture" (1993a, 289). In this sense, the great stories of our tradition often radiate conceptions of vulnerability, belongingness, and dependency that invariably clash with the modern values of individualism. And in the process of hermeneutic psychotherapy, they illuminate a deeper understanding of the historical context that grounds our contemporary experiences of isolation and rage, opening up new ways to interpret and make sense of who we are and what ought to matter in our lives.

Of course, the difficulty in revising our current self-understanding, as Heidegger makes clear, is that the cultural prejudices that constitute American individualism are so much a part of us that we are largely unaware of how we embody and enact them in our everyday lives. They are "not only close to us—even which is closest; *we are it*, each of us, we ourselves" (BT, 15, my emphasis). As long as psychiatry continues to treat the human being as a decontextualized object, where the aim of treatment is to alter biochemistry and provide techniques to effectively cope with the stresses and frustrations of American life, the "historicality" (*Geschichtlichkeit*) and meaning-structures that shape our current self-understanding will never be addressed. This is why hermeneutic psychiatry is suspicious of the overuse of impersonal and instrumental words like *effectiveness, technique, mechanism,* and *skill* that, in clinical practice, have become the equivalent to "God terms" (Richardson 2012). It recognizes that scientific technique reaches its limit when it enters the domain of mental illness because this is not simply a domain of neurological or cognitive processes but of historical meanings, cultural values, and human relationships. Regardless of how advanced neuroscience, molecular genetics, or brain imaging technology becomes, it will never help us understand the *meaning* of a person's suffering. Thus, when Heidegger claims that, "a bare subject without a world never 'is' firstly, nor is it ever given" (BT, 116), he is helping to scrap the myth that our psychic pain somehow resides inside the mind or brain. Human existence, as being-in-the-world, is structurally "ex-static"; we are already "standing outside" ourselves with others, embedded in a shared culture and history. And the meaning of a person's experience can be grasped only by situating suffering within that context. In this way, hermeneutic psychiatry is not so concerned with treating the functional symptoms of mental illness but with empathically attending to the person's way of being-in-the-world in an attempt to understand the meanings that hold that way of being together. Without this kind of therapeutic orientation, the long-term outcomes for the patient remain bleak. Heidegger makes it clear that opening up the patient to this kind of deep contextual self-understanding ought to be the primary aim of healing. "As to the physician's will-to-help," he writes, "one must pay attention that it involves a *way of being* and not the *functioning* of some*thing*. If one only aims at the latter,

then one does not add to [the understanding] of Dasein. *But this is the goal.*"
And insofar as we close ourselves off from the edifying stories of our past,
we will remain trapped and alone in the present, in the isolating paradigm of
ontological individualism, experiencing a "loss of freedom [and] a constriction of the possibility of living" (ZS1, 157, my emphasis).

NOTE

1. The primary exceptions to this in Dostoevsky's corpus are the characters of Alyosha
Karamazov in *The Brothers Karamazov* and Prince Myshkin in *The Idiot*. Both characters serve
as heroic, antimodern figures guided by the Christ-like values of innocence, community, and
compassion, serving as embodiments of the Eastern Church.

Afterword

The ideas laid out in this book are very personal to me, as I have struggled with depression and anxiety for much of my adult life. The cycles of rumination, the obsessive "what ifs," the insomnia, and the affective narrowing of spatial and temporal horizons are all too familiar to me. I have benefited greatly from various psychiatric medications, psychotherapies, and mindfulness-based practices to manage my dark moods. Indeed, without the help of the antidepressant Celexa, I very much doubt I would have finished my PhD and gone on to have a modestly successful academic career. But more than the pills and therapies, it has been teaching and writing about existentialism and phenomenology, especially the work of Heidegger, over the last two decades that has helped me make sense of and contextualize my experience. For me, Heidegger's analytic of Dasein not only provides the conceptual tools to understand what it means *to be* human; more importantly, it illuminates what it means and what it feels like when our capacity *to be* breaks down. I have had many students approach me after lecturing on Heidegger's account of anxiety confessing that his descriptions of breakdown and world-collapse powerfully capture their own experiences. And they often discuss how they too don't feel "at home" in this world, how they have difficulty fitting in or cohering with the American values of hyperindividualism, ruthless competition, and self-promotion and how this leaves them feeling overwhelmed, isolated, and confused about how to live. To this end, Heidegger's thought has provided me, as well as many of my students, with a sense of recognition and acknowledgment of our own suffering. This is why, in my view, so many are initially drawn to Heidegger's thought in the first place; it transcends the narrow terrain of academic philosophy by illuminating the unique pain of being human and situating this pain within the human condition itself. Indeed, after many years working alongside him during the *Zolli-*

119

kon Seminars, Medard Boss became convinced that this is how Heidegger had envisioned his intellectual contribution all along. "He saw the possibility that his philosophical insights would not be confined merely to the philosopher's quarters but also might be of benefit to wider circles, in particular to a large number of suffering human beings" (2001, xvii).

In closing, I want to try to bring the core ideas of this book together by offering a phenomenological case study that draws on my own personal experience following a massive heart attack in December 2018. The aim of this narrative is to concretize the richness and depth of Heidegger's insights in a way that is free of any obfuscating jargon. By disclosing the different ways in which the experiential structures of my being broke down in the aftermath of the event, I try to expose the limits of the biomedical paradigm and highlight how important it is to be acknowledged and recognized by health-care professionals as a person who is suffering and scared rather than simply a malfunctioning physical body. This kind of existential recognition has provided a skein of meanings that I have been able to draw on to gradually refashion my being in the midst of cognitive and emotional wreckage. More importantly, it has temporarily opened me up to reservoirs of vulnerability and compassion that were largely concealed when I was healthy and absorbed in the routines of everyday life. This, for me, has been the hidden gift of the illness; it illuminates the universality of pain, suffering, and death, of our fundamental helplessness and dependency on others, and of the vital role human connections play in healing.

MY HEART ATTACK

It was a beautiful December day in Southwest Florida, a Saturday, bright sun, blue sky, low humidity. I planned a sixty-mile solo bike ride around the town of Estero, the Fort Myers Airport, and the neighboring communities of Gateway, Treeline, and Colonial. Finishing up the ride in around three-and-a-half hours, I rode over the Estero Bridge to my house, when I was suddenly overcome with nausea and lightheadedness. I slammed on the brakes, threw my bike to the ground, and vomited all over the street. Confused and thinking I had food poisoning or overdid it on the ride, I slowly pedaled back home. Then the chest pain came as a dull, persistent ache. I called my girlfriend, telling her that I was having some trouble. She said it sounded like I was having a heart attack. I dismissed it. "No, I'm just hungry and dehydrated and need to take a shower." She raced to my house and convinced me to go to the emergency room as the dizziness deepened. A quick EKG ushered me into a suite of scurrying doctors and nurses who were already preparing for the surgery. All I heard from the din was "Massive Heart Attack . . . LAD blocked . . . Code Stent . . . Code Stent!" This was the beginning.

A week after the heart attack was Christmas Day, and I was feeling much better. Always physically active, my girlfriend and I now committed to a heart healthy diet and were preparing meals at home for the first time in our relationship. I had walked five miles during the day and took a hot bath in the evening. I was returning to my old self again, more quickly than I could have imagined. I would be healthy and whole before the start of the spring semester. The next day, I started out on my morning walk but only got to the end of the driveway. My right calf felt tight and achy, and my toes were numb. I came back to the house with a grim "Something's wrong." We rushed back to the hospital, where I received an ultrasound on my leg, and sure enough, a blood clot was in a major artery. Three days of treatment with a vascular surgeon, angiograms to examine the clot, and various tubes inserted through my left groin down to my right calf. (The right groin couldn't be used, as that was the side they had gone up to place the stent.) The surgeon was unable to suck the clot out with a tiny vacuum, so he opted for an aggressive intravenous clot buster treatment combined with high doses of a blood thinner. I was unable to eat or stand for the duration. Every hour, the nurse would measure the size of my calf to see if blood was flowing, and each hour I was gripped with terror that it was getting larger or that the pulse in my right foot was getting weaker. Each night was a din of buzzers, beeps, blood tests, and vital sign checks. I slept in fits and starts. This was the beginning.

I was finally released from intensive care after the clot buster medication had done its work, and I was able to move to my own hospital room for observation. Having my own bathroom, a window, and the ability to eat solid food was succor. The diagnosis was that a clot in my heart had been discharged during the heart attack, and that I would need to be on a battery of blood thinners to prevent future clots from forming. This was bad but not terrible. I could take the medications, go to cardiac rehabilitation, and get back to my normal routine in no time. On the second night of observation, an alarm and flashing red light erupted from the heart monitor hanging on the wall. A thirty-second burst of ventricular tachycardia. Now things got complicated. The next morning the cardiologist warned that I may be susceptible to sudden cardiac death and needed to see an electro-cardiologist to determine the extent of the problem. But the test, involving electrodes placed on the heart to induce tachycardia, could not be done because of concern that it would dislodge the clot in my heart and lead to a possible stroke. The solution was to wear a portable defibrillator (or life vest) for two months as the clot dissolved and then decide whether or not to implant a defibrillator in my chest. I was stricken with the reality that the heart attack and the various complications had left me with a profoundly altered body. I am now forced to confront the possibility that reclaiming my former self is not an option. This is the beginning.

MY ALTERED BODY

To have a massive heart attack at the age of 48, at what I thought was the prime of my life, has been nothing less than world shattering. The visceral awareness of the frailty and vulnerability of my body and the recognition of my fundamental dependency on others have trashed the illusions of my own strength and autonomy. But the experience has also concretized insights in existential philosophy and the phenomenology of the body that I have been reading and writing about for years, revealing a now intimate understanding of critical illness and the limitations of mainstream biomedicine. Again, the signature contribution of phenomenology when it comes to body ailments is the way in which it brackets out or suspends the detached perspective of scientific medicine, focusing instead on the lived-experience of the suffering individual. To this end, phenomenology is not concerned with identifying a causal explanation of my heart attack through the technical use of echocardiograms, X-rays, or blood tests. Instead, the aim is to arrive at a contextual understanding of the experience. Thus, the phenomenologist is concerned with the experience of illness *as it is lived*, to understand it, situate it, and give it meaning. By closely attending to experience in this way, the intent is to return to "the things themselves," to the structures of meaning that constitute our subjectivity and the way these structures are altered and break down in illness. This requires an alternative to the way in which biomedicine interprets the body.

What became clear in the aftermath of the heart attack is that the physicians and surgeons rarely encountered me as a person. I was reduced to numerical data, to numbers and sets of numbers revealed through various diagnostic instruments. I was a 45–50 percent ejection fraction; an INR of 5.7; an S/P sustained 83 VTACH; or an ST > 0.15V. For every procedure or blood test, I was not Kevin Aho, a middle-aged philosophy professor with parents who were worried about him, with two loving brothers, a girlfriend, and a career that he cared deeply about, who was now struggling and overwhelmed in the face of a collapsing world. There was little attempt to listen to the person behind the symptoms. I was simply a corporeal thing, an object of measurement. And this pattern of measuring blood pressure, temperature, pulse, and respiration rates took place every four hours for twelve straight days, pulling me out of deep sleep every night at 2 am. Each time I was poked and prodded, my rest and recovery was interrupted, leaving me frustrated and exhausted. It seemed as if the health-care professionals saw my body as something "*I have*" rather than who "*I am*." They were unfamiliar with Heidegger's words, that "we do not 'have' a body; rather, *we 'are' bodily . . . we are somebody who is alive*" (N, 99). Moreover, the numbers gathered from these measurements were not impersonal facts. They meant something to me, pointing toward what kind of life I can live, whether or not I can ride my bike again, travel overseas, or flourish in my profession.

From the standpoint of my own experience, my body is not a corporeal thing that the physician examines from a standpoint of cool detachment. It is *my body* and the panoply of experiences, feeling, and meanings that belong to me. As Gabriel Marcel writes, "what I feel is indissolubly linked to the fact that my body is *my body*, not just one body among others. . . . Nobody who is not inside my skin can know what I feel" (1950, 104). But understanding the body in this way requires more than being attentive to the first-person experiences of the patient. Phenomenologists also acknowledge the importance of the mediating activity of our physiology and the perceptual and postural systems that prereflectively orient and situate us in the world. When I was healthy, these sensory-motor systems remained hidden in the background, opening up the practical horizon or space of my life and seamlessly coordinating my movements and position in relation to the vertical ("up and down"), the horizontal ("front and back") and other axes. This mediating activity constituted a tacit sense of "I can" as I engaged in the familiar habits and patterns of everyday life. With my heart attack, these transparent functions collapsed, and the corporeal body emerged out of its hiddenness. I became aware of my body as an object, as something foreign and strange. Every pinch in my chest, every constricted breath and skipped heartbeat pulled me away from the "I can" and injected doubt and worry into everything I did, resulting in a profound alteration to the structures of meaning that constitute who I am.

SPATIAL WOUNDS

From the perspective of my own experience, space is not encountered as a three-dimensional coordinate system. It is, rather, the experiential horizon that opens up in the course of my daily activities. Before my heart attack, this horizon was expansive and was constituted effortlessly by simply moving through the world. Taken-for-granted activities like driving, walking, negotiating stairs, giving a lecture, or picking up and handling objects were performed in a smooth and transparent way, and this held open and broadened the space of my everyday concerns. In the aftermath of the heart attack, this space quickly closed in on me. I vividly recall the yellow footprints painted on the floor of my hospital room that ran from the bed to the bathroom. There were four footprints in all with a sign on the door that read, "Walking helps your recovery." When I asked the nurse what this meant, she said it refers to the importance of walking to the bathroom. In the span of a few days, the horizon of my life had shrunk from sixty-mile bike rides to four steps. I felt as if I had moved from *Leib* to *Körper*, from the effortless activity of making space to merely occupying space as a corporeal thing.

This experience of spatial collapse didn't end when I was discharged from the hospital. There were constant reminders of my new limits. A kind of agoraphobia set in. The neighborhood streets in the evening seemed threatening, especially when my house was no longer in view. A drive to the grocery store or to work took on frightening implications. And flying to a new city for a conference or to visit friends and family seemed impossible. The collapse was so acute that I asked my younger brother to come stay with me for a few days when my girlfriend was out of town for work, fearing that I'd be unable to leave the house. There were also more subtle reminders. The bike rack on the roof of my car continued to haunt me, indicating the loss of strength and independence. Social media feeds on Facebook and Instagram were filled with photos of smiling faces, dinners with friends, exotic locations, and ski outings, all suggesting how narrow and constricted the space of my life had become. When looking out my office windows, I watched young students playing Frisbee on the lawn, riding their skateboards and laughing as if to remind me of my new frailty. Even the architectural design of the built environment seemed like a spatial betrayal. The stairs to my office or to my car in the parking garage left me short of breath, the long boardwalk, the distance to the library were all signs, were all whispering of my weakness. The "I can" that opened up my world, that I effortlessly embodied just a few weeks earlier, had become a debilitating "I can't."

TEMPORAL WOUNDS

Before my heart attack, the future was expansive and filled with worthwhile projects shaped by a past that was grounded in physical strength, self-confidence, and a generally upbeat temperament. I was running toward a future of continued health and professional success, of travel and writing, of cultivating new friendships and sustaining old ones. There was a sense of integrity and solidity to who I was because the meanings and interpretations I projected for myself were coherent and bound together with my past. My illness shattered the illusion of this temporal unity, exposing an arrested future of medical tests and hospital visits, of medications and monitoring. When the future collapsed in this way, the resources of the past that I relied on to create my identity no longer held, and I was left to confront the ultimate question, "*Who am I*"? I was no longer the productive professor, the cyclist, or the skier. These former identities no longer made sense to me in the wake of the heart attack. My future projects shifted from writing a new book or traveling to France with my girlfriend to walking to the bathroom without losing my breath. I felt as if the future and the past were closing in on me, as if I were trapped in a meaningless present, left to the moment-to-moment rituals of taking medication, checking my blood pressure and pulse, and arranging the next doctor visit.

An atmosphere of depression and emptiness began to color my life. Things that I used to take pleasure in, watching a good movie, reading the *New York Times* on Sunday, or enjoying a nice meal, now revealed themselves as affectively empty and flat. The plot line and dialogue of the movie was unintelligible, the words in the newspaper article were confusing and disjointed, and food was bland and tasteless. My post–heart attack mood revealed a bleached-out world, where the things that I encountered and handled every day were, with few exceptions, affectively meaningless. As a result, the activities that used to stand out as significant for me, the very things I drew on to construct a unified and coherent self-interpretation, imploded. The heart attack disrupted the future-directed understanding that I had of my life, undermined the constitutive meanings of my past, and left me in a state of limbo, unable *to be*.

HERMENEUTIC WOUNDS

The language of medical expertise had a profound impact on me. "Ischemic cardiomyopathy," "myocardial infarction," or "coronary artery disease" are not merely diagnostic labels; they were vital symbols that reflected my situation and that I had to draw on to create a new identity. Viewing me from the dispassionate lens of biomedicine, the physicians and surgeons seemed largely oblivious to the power of their own words. After I was admitted back into intensive care with a blood clot, I remember an especially callous doctor telling me: "It may require surgery, but who knows?" I remember hanging on these words and replying angrily, "You should know! You're the damn doctor." After my episode of ventricular tachycardia, a cardiologist entered my hospital room and said that I am now at risk of sudden cardiac death and may need to have a defibrillator implanted in my chest. The words "sudden death" and "defibrillator" left me reeling. Before I had a chance to comprehend this news, to ask, "What does this mean for me?" and "How am I going to live?" he was already walking briskly down the hall. A few days later, another cardiologist came to my room and said I would need to wear a life-vest for the next two months. Again, the very word "life-vest" darkened my future, dimming my capacity for self-creation.

The medical terms that captured my diagnosis closed down my sense of futurity, but they also corrupted my past. Experiences of strength, confidence, and vitality that were so much a part of my identity before the heart attack suddenly seemed foreign, as if they belonged to someone else, and the future revealed itself as a horizon of weakness and futility, one that was confined to the medical industrial complex. And the detached discourse of health-care professionals only exacerbated the experience, turning me into a passive object and stripping away any sense of agency. Physicians would often discuss my condition from the third person perspective in front of me, as if I weren't even in the room. "Patient was treated with beta blockers and an ace-inhibitor." "Patient's pulse is brady." "Patient was transferred to the cath lab." The focus was on treatment rather than healing, on *what* was being done to my corporeal body rather than *who* was living or undergoing the treatments. When I would ask for clarification regarding the significance of these various treatments in an attempt to understand them, I was dismissed. It became clear that it was not even the physicians but the technology itself that was the authority. The physicians deferred not to me, not to how I felt, but to the data transmitted on the heart monitor, the X-ray, or the ultrasound. Any attempt on my part to intervene in the sheer instrumentality of the proceedings appeared to be viewed as a disruption in the delivery of care. The overall impact of this objectification was a feeling of profound helplessness, that I was no longer a participant in my own existence.

RELATIONAL WOUNDS

Before my heart attack, I was absorbed in the relational flow of the world, seamlessly engaging with public life and the various roles and practices that fortified my sense of self. I was invisible, able to disappear or vanish into the web of social relations. But illness disturbed this synchronous flow and made me visible. I was now too slow and clumsy on the staircase, unable to keep up on walks to the library or finish a three-hour lecture in the afternoon. Without the ability to disappear into ordinary social situations, I felt as if I was, in Sartre's words, a "body-for-others" (*corps pour autrui*), an object under the gaze of the healthy and normal. The experience of myself as a body-for-others was magnified when I had to start wearing the life-vest. Although the external defibrillator was largely concealed under my shirt, it was attached to a camera-sized box at my hip, with a black cord running up my side. It was unmistakably a medical device, and I felt the stigma. When colleagues would approach me, they would glance at the device and ask with concern, "How are you doing?" and "Is everything alright?"—questions that inflamed my sense of brokenness. What was especially disturbing is that some colleagues whom I considered friends before the illness appeared to avoid me altogether or would simply smile and scurry away, perhaps uncomfortable with what I represented: shattered health, vulnerability, and a reminder of death. Others, after asking about my condition, would redirect the conversations back to themselves, describing their excellent cholesterol levels, lack of heart disease in the family, fitness regimen, or the value of their plant-based or vegan diet. Through all of this, the gaze of the other branded me as ill, as an outsider, as someone who disrupted a tacit social harmony. And all of this made me acutely aware of my altered body. I began to internalize the judgment of others, to see myself as they saw me. In an effort to avoid judgment, I would try to disguise my condition. I would present myself as healthy, upbeat, and strong when colleagues or students came to the office; I would hide my medical device on my lap or carry it over my shoulder like a fashion accessory; I would make up excuses about why I couldn't attend a meeting or event; I would pretend to take a phone call if I felt tired or overwhelmed. All of this was done in an effort to disappear, to vanish back into the flow of everydayness.

HEALING THE ALTERED BODY

Heidegger refers to illness in terms of "a loss of freedom, [and] a constriction of the possibility of living" (ZS1, 157). For me, this constriction took a number of forms, from spatial and temporal collapse to a narrowing of narrative possibilities and relational ways of being. Each of these represented a disruption or breakdown in the structures of meaning that constitute my being. Healing involves becoming receptive and open to the world once again, to projecting new possibilities and meanings against the background of the illness. This process is taking place slowly, beginning with simple movements. From being bedridden, to being able to stand, to walking down the hospital corridor a few days later, to walking around the block, to walking several miles, these incremental expressions of motility began to create a new foundation for my experience of lived-space. A horizon that consisted of a hospital bed for weeks began to gradually widen and expand. Instead of just "taking up" space as a corporeal object, my capacity for movement allowed me to "make space" once again. When I was cleared to drive, when I walked across campus to my office for the first time, when I taught my afternoon seminar, when I made love again, the space of concerns continued to broaden. But this spatial broadening is tentative. There is persistent fear of another incident, a pain in the chest or a blood clot that will send me back to the constricted confines of the illness.

Disruption of the temporal structure of my existence has made it difficult to project myself toward a meaningful future. In the immediate aftermath of the heart attack, I was not only absorbed in the moment-to-moment management of my own limitations and despair, but it was also unclear to me how I could draw on the discursive resources of my past. It was as if the heart attack had established a new starting point, a new foundation for my life going forward. Any meaningful identity that I could envision was now constrained by the illness. And I would have to work against the background of these constraints to create myself again. Again, this process of reopening the future has been gradual. I've had to slough off identities that no longer hold for me. The most obvious is letting go of the sense of myself as someone who is fit, athletic, and strong. Physical fitness had been integral to who I am since I was a teenager and provided a decades-long release from chronic anxiety. Running, cycling, and lifting weights at the gym were all like therapy. They calmed me down, released endorphins, and fortified my confidence and feeling of well-being. With the heart attack as my new birthplace, the meanings of fitness have shifted dramatically. At least for the time being, I have to make do with slowness and being patient, with walking, stretching, and meditation, letting go of the past, and acknowledging that there are many different ways to interpret the idea of strength.

My identity as a professor has also changed. I had long fashioned myself a productive scholar and an energetic teacher and colleague, but that energy and enthusiasm is diminished both by the illness as well as by the various heart and arrhythmia medications that make me light-headed and easily fatigued. Long days at the office or marathon writing sessions are difficult, and I have been forced to say "no" to projects and trips that I would normally jump on. This has all created tentativeness about my future as a professor. It feels uncertain, filled with ruminations. Will I be able to travel if I am implanted with a defibrillator? How will I cope if or when the device shocks me? What will my next echocardiogram reveal about the health of my heart? How will this affect my ability to do my job? Much of my energy is devoted to managing this kind apprehension, a fear that narrows and constricts the possibilities available to me. But with each day at the office, with every hour I spend in front of my students, with each word I type for a new manuscript, the future opens up a little more. In the process, I am recognizing that I have to be flexible, that I cannot cling to my former self-interpretation, and that I have to let go of identities that are no longer livable.

The pain of letting go or giving up on my former self was not made any easier by the physicians who largely seemed oblivious to my experience, confined as they were in the objectifying discourse of biomedicine. But there were some in the hospital, fellow sufferers, who listened to me, affirming and accepting my experience. Their attentiveness to me as a lived-body rather than a corporeal thing opened up new meanings that have helped me refashion my life-story, with my illness now serving as a foundational chapter. There was a particularly dark moment in the hospital when my cardiologist had diagnosed ventricular tachycardia, the possibility of sudden cardiac death, and the possible need for a defibrillator. A nursing assistant came in a few minutes later and sang a negro spiritual to lift my mood and let me touch her scar from her own pacemaker. She talked openly about wanting to commit suicide earlier in her life, of her congenital heart trouble and getting her pacemaker at forty. I was overcome by her compassion, by her capacity to see me as someone who was frightened. Then there was the nurse from the intensive care unit, who confessed to his own cardiac issues from atrial fibrillation and spoke honestly about his anxiety and how he would have to give himself positive affirmations in front of the mirror in the morning in order to leave the house and go to work. Another nurse stopped by my room after a procedure, saw that I was frightened, and disclosed that he had cystic fibrosis and probably not long to live, but that his life was still worth living. And there was a young nurse, a former student of mine, who quietly told me one evening that she entered the healing professions to confront the pain of losing her father to colon cancer.

Each of these disclosures provided the recognition I desperately needed and offered a discursive context that I could draw on to express and make sense of my shattered identity. From these encounters, the interpretive structure of my existence remained intact, and I was, against the backdrop of my illness, able to envision a future that could still be meaningful and fulfilling. This highlights the importance of situating and acknowledging the existential suffering of the patient as fundamental to healing. The fact that those who listened to and affirmed my experience were mostly nurses (or nursing assistants) reveals something about the instrumental and transactional nature of modern doctoring, where the aim is not to listen and tend to a particular person but to manage and treat malfunctioning body parts. Many physicians, including Dr. Bernard Lown, the cardiologist and inventor of the very defibrillator that I thought I would be implanted with, have critiqued the industrialization of their profession for this reason. Today, writes Lown, "healing is replaced by treating, caring is supplanted by managing, and the art of listening is taken over by technological procedures" (1999, xiv). For me, without others listening to and caring about my situation, there would be no healing and, consequently, no way to project a meaningful path forward.

This aspect of healing, of being recognized and accepted as a person who was suffering, exposed deeper layers of relationality, revealing the fundamental vulnerability at the core of the human condition. When I was healthy and caught up in the flow of everyday life, this vulnerability remained largely closed off to me. But the heart attack cracked me open. I was suddenly overflowing, not just with anxiety but also with love and compassion. I called my brothers weeping shortly after the angioplasty, telling them how much I cared about them and how thankful I was to have them in my life. My girlfriend became my fiancée in the intensive care unit after my blood clot. I felt as if I were seeing her for the first time with fresh eyes, as the beautiful, courageous, and tender being that she is. My parents, whom I spoke to everyday, revealed themselves in all of their generosity and devotion to their broken son. The people in my life that I ordinarily took for granted became luminous and fragile. And this extended beyond my family, partner, and intimate friends to include colleagues, neighbors, and even complete strangers at the supermarket or gas station. The masks came off, and I sensed how helpless and dependent we all are, and this made me care even more. The experience feels analogous to what Emmanuel Levinas described as "the face" (*le visage*), when the other reveals him or herself not as a thing but as a pure expression of nudity, defenselessness and vulnerability (1969, 199). This expression for Levinas not only illuminates *who we really are* beneath the stable crust of everyday social convention but also issues a command or plea to take responsibility and care for each other.

This feeling of being cracked open has been the gift of the illness. As I struggle with the limitations of my altered body, let go of a former self that is no longer livable, and work to refashion a new identity in the face of a precarious and restricted future, I am grateful for what the heart attack has taught me. I recognize now that I am not, and never have been, a masterful and autonomous subject, that I am fundamentally defenseless and dependent on others. And the recognition of our shared vulnerability is healing insofar as it binds us together in the wake of pain and loss, reminding us that we are not alone in our suffering. To this end, Heidegger's insights have not only allowed me to see how the constitutive meaning-structures of my experience can break down but also how they can be rebuilt. The way in which our existence is structured, by space and time, by our capacity to interpret and give meaning to the world, and by our intersubjectivity, are always vulnerable to collapse. Illness reminds us of this. But, insofar as our suffering is not just treated with medical technology but *heard, acknowledged*, and *affirmed* by others, there is still a way forward; there is still joy in being alive.

References

Abbey, S., and Garfinkel, P. 1991. Neurasthenia and chronic fatigue syndrome: The role of culture in the making of a diagnosis. *American journal of psychiatry* 148(12): 1638–46.

Aho, J., and Aho, K. 2008. *Body matters: A phenomenology of sickness, illness, and disease*. Lanham, MD: Lexington Books.

Aho, K. 2007. Acceleration and time pathologies: The critique of psychology in Heidegger's *Beiträge*. *Time and society* 16(1): 25–42.

Aho, K. 2009. *Heidegger's neglect of the body*. Albany, NY: SUNY Press.

Aho, K. 2016. Kierkegaard on boredom and self-loss in the age of online dating. In M. Gardiner and J. J. Haladyn (eds.), *Boredom studies reader*. London: Routledge.

Aho, K., and Guignon, C. 2011. Medicalized psychiatry and the talking cure: A hermeneutic intervention. *Human studies: A journal for philosophy and the social sciences* 34: 293–308.

Alvarez, A. 1990. *The savage god: A study of suicide*. New York: W. W. Norton.

American Psychiatric Association (APA). 1952. *Diagnostic and statistical manual of mental disorders* (DSM-I). Washington, DC: American Psychiatric Association.

American Psychiatric Association (APA). 1968. *Diagnostic and statistical manual of mental disorders* (DSM-II). Washington, DC: American Psychiatric Association.

American Psychiatric Association (APA). 1980. *Diagnostic and statistical manual of mental disorders* (DSM-III). Washington, DC: American Psychiatric Association.

American Psychiatric Association (APA). 1994. *Diagnostic and statistical manual of mental disorders* (DSM-IV). Washington, DC: American Psychiatric Association.

American Psychiatric Association (APA.) 2000. *Diagnostic and statistical manual of mental disorders, text revised* (DSM-IV TR). Washington, DC: American Psychiatric Association.

American Psychiatric Association (APA). 2013. *Diagnostic and statistical manual of mental disorders* (DSM-V). Washington, DC: American Psychiatric Association.

Andreasen, N. 1985. *The broken brain: The biological revolution in psychiatry*. New York: Harper and Row.

Angell, M. 2011a. The epidemic of mental illness: Why? *New York Review of Books*, July 23.

Angell, M. 2011b. The illusions of psychiatry. *New York Review of Books*, July 1.

Antrim, D. 2019. Everywhere and nowhere: A night on the roof and a suicide averted. *The New Yorker*, February 18–25, 68–77.

Aronowitz, R. 1991. Lyme disease: the social construction of a new disease and its social consequences. *The milbank quarterly* 69(1): 79–112.

Ash, P. 1949. The reliability of psychiatric diagnosis. *Journal of abnormal and social psychology* 44: 272–76.

Askey, R. 2001. Heidegger's philosophy and its implications for psychology, Freud, and existential psychoanalysis. In M. Heidegger, *Zollikon seminars: Protocols—conversations—letters*. Evanston, IL: Northwestern University Press.

Barford, V. 2016. Why are Americans so angry? *BBC news*. https://www.bbc.com/news/magazine-35406324. Accessed December 16, 2018.

Barker, K. 2009. *The fibromyalgia story: Medical authority and women's worlds of pain*. Philadelphia, PA: Temple University Press.

Beard, G. 1880. *A practical treatise on nervous exhaustion (neurasthenia)*. New York: William Wood.

Beard, G. 1881. *American nervousness, its causes and consequences: A supplement to nervous exhaustion (neurasthenia)*. New York: G. P. Putnam's Sons.

Beck, U. 1992. *Risk society: Towards a new modernity*. London: Sage.

Bellah, R. et al. 1985. *Habits of the heart: Individualism and commitment in American life*. Berkeley: University of California Press.

Benedict, C. 2006. What's wrong with a child? Psychiatrists often disagree. *New York Times*, November 11. https://www.nytimes.com/2006/11/11/health/psychology/11kids.html?mtrref=www.google.com&gwh=24DEE7FC86AE913687AAB806DA63A807&gwt=pay. Accessed November 20, 2018.

Blackman, L. 2001. *Hearing voices: Embodiment and experience*. London: Free Association Books.

Blattner, W. 1994. The concept of death in *Being and Time*. *Man and world* 27: 49–70.

Blattner, W. 2009. *Heidegger's* Being and Time. New York: London: Continuum.

Blazer, D. 2005. *The age of melancholy: 'Major depression' and its social origin*. New York: Routledge.

Boss. M. 2001. Preface to the first German edition of Martin Heidegger's Zollikon Seminars. In M. Boss (ed.), *Martin Heidegger: Zollikon seminars, protocols—conversation—letters*. Trans. F. Mayr and R. Askay. Evanston, IL: Northwestern University Press.

Boss, M. 2019. A memoir. Trans. M. Groth. *Existential analysis* 30(1): 169–98.

Boulton, T. 2018. Nothing and everything: Fibromyalgia as a diagnosis of exclusion and inclusion. *Qualitative health research*. DOI: 10.1177/104973231880409.

Bracken, P. 2014. Toward a hermeneutic shift in psychiatry. *World psychiatry* 13(3): 241–43.

Bracken, P., and Thomas, P. 2005. *Postpsychiatry: Mental health in the postmodern world*. New York: Oxford University Press.

Breggin, P. 1994. *Toxic psychiatry: Why therapy, empathy and love must replace the drugs, electroshock, and biochemical theories of the 'new psychiatry.'* New York: St. Martin's Griffin.

Byung-Chul, H. 2015. *The burnout society*. Stanford, CA: Stanford University Press.

Cain, S. 2012. *Quiet: The power of introverts in a world that can't stop talking*. New York: Broadway Books.

Caputo, J. 1994. *Sorge* and *kardia*: The hermeneutics of factical life and the categories of the heart. In T. Kisiel and J. van Buren (eds.), *Reading Heidegger from the start: Essays in his earliest thought*. Albany, NY: SUNY Press.

Carlat, D. 2011. The illusions of psychiatry: An exchange. *New York Review of Books*, August 18.

Carman, T. 2003. *Heidegger's analytic: Interpretation, discourse, and authenticity in* Being and Time. Cambridge: Cambridge University Press.

Carver, R. 1998. *Where I'm calling from: Selected stories*. New York: Atlantic Monthly Press.

Cederström, C. 2018. *The happiness fantasy*. Cambridge: Polity.

Cerbone, D. 2000. Heidegger and Dasein's 'bodily nature': What is the hidden problematic. *International journal of philosophical studies* 8(2): 209–30.

Chalmers, D. 1996. *The conscious mind: In search of a fundamental theory*. New York: Oxford University Press.

Charmaz, K. 1983. The loss of self: A fundamental form of suffering in the chronically ill. *Sociology of health and illness* 52(2): 168–95.

Chatel, J., and Peele, R. 1970. The concept of neurasthenia. *International journal of psychiatry* 9: 36–49.

Chodoff, P. 2002. The medicalization of the human condition. *Psychiatric service* 53(5): 627–28.

Coccaro, E. 2015. Intermittent explosive disorder. *Psychiatric times* 32(3): 1–3.

Cohn, Hans. 1997. *Existential thought and therapeutic practice: An introduction to existential psychotherapy.* London: Sage.

Conrad, P. 2007. *The medicalization of society: On the transformation of human conditions into treatable disorders.* Baltimore, MD: The Johns Hopkins University Press.

Cottle, M. 1999. Selling shyness. *The New Republic*, August 2.

Cushman, P. 1995. *Constructing the self, constructing America: A cultural history of psychotherapy.* New York: Da Capo Press.

Cushman, P. 2003. How psychology erodes personhood. *Journal of theoretical and philosophical psychology* 22: 103–13.

Cushman, P., and Gilford, P. 2000. Will managed care change our way of being? *American psychologist* 55(9): 985–96.

Davis, L. 2008. *Obsession: A history.* Chicago: University of Chicago Press.

Dilthey, W. 1958. Der Aufbau der Geschichtlichen Welt in den Geisteswissenschaften. In W. Dilthey, *Gesammelte schriften, Vol. VIII.* Stuttgart: B. G. Teubner.

Dilthey, W. 2002. *Formation of the historical world in the human sciences.* R. Makkreel and F. Rodi (eds.). Princeton, NJ: Princeton University Press.

Dorman, L. 2001. Planet no. In N. Casey (ed.), *Unholy ghost.* New York: Harper Perennial.

Dostoevsky, F. 1957. *The brothers Karamazov.* Trans. C. Garnett. New York: New American Library.

Dostoevsky, F. 1968. *Crime and punishment.* Trans. S. Monas. New York: New American Library.

Dostoevsky, F. 2009. *Notes from the underground.* Trans. C. Garnett. Indianapolis, IN: Hackett.

Dreyfus, H. 1990. *Being-in-the-world: A commentary on Heidegger's* Being and Time, *Division I.* Cambridge, MA: MIT Press.

Drinka, G. 1984. *The birth of neurosis: Myth, malady, and the Victorians.* New York: Simon and Schuster.

Dugin, A. 2017. Plural anthropology (the fundamental-ontological analysis of peoples). In J. Love (ed.), *Heidegger in Russia and Eastern Europe.* London: Rowman & Littlefield International.

Duhigg, C. 2019. The real roots of American rage: The untold story of how anger became the dominant emotion in our politics and our personal lives—and what we can do about it. *The Atlantic.* https://www.theatlantic.com/magazine/archive/2019/01/charles-duhigg-american-anger/576424/. Accessed April 10, 2019.

Ehrenreich, B. 2009. *Bright-sided: How positive thinking is undermining America.* New York: Picador.

Elliott, C. 2010. The secret lives of big pharma's 'thought leaders.' *The chronicle of higher education.* September 12. https://www.chronicle.com/article/The-Secret-Lives-of-Big/124335. Accessed September 12, 2018.

Elliott, C. 2016. Pursued by happiness and beaten senseless: Prozac and the American dream. In C. Elliott and T. Chambers (eds.), *Prozac as a way of life.* Chapel Hill: University of North Carolina Press.

Ellis, B. 1991. *American psycho.* New York: Vintage.

Elpidorou, A., and Freeman, L. 2015. Affectivity in Heidegger I: Moods and emotions in *Being and Time. Philosophy compass* 10(10): 661–71.

Frank, A. 1991. *At the will of the body: reflections on illness.* New York: Houghton Mifflin Company.

Fraser, M. 2001. The nature of Prozac. *History of the human sciences* 14(3): 56–84.

Freedman, A. 1987. Introduction. *Before Freud: Neurasthenia and the American medical community, 1870-1910.* Urbana: University of Illinois Press.

Freeman, M. 2002. When the story's over: Narrative foreclosure and the possibility of self-renewal. In M. Andrews et al. (eds.), *Lines of narrative: Psychosocial perspectives.* London: Routledge.

Frie, R. 1997. *Subjectivity and intersubjectivity in modern philosophy and psychoanalysis: A study of Sartre, Binswanger, Lacan, and Habermas*. Lanham, MD: Rowman & Littlefield.

Fuchs, T. 2003. The phenomenology of shame, guilt, and the body in body dysmorphic disorder and depression. *Journal of phenomenological psychology* 33(2): 223–43.

Fuchs, T. 2005a. The phenomenology of the body, space and time in depression. *Comprendre* 15: 108–21.

Fuchs, T. 2005b. Delusional mood and delusional perception—a phenomenological analysis. *Psychopathology* 38: 133–39.

Fuchs, T. 2005c. Corporealized and disembodied minds: A phenomenological view of the body in melancholia and schizophrenia. *Philosophy, psychiatry, and psychology* 12(2): 95–107.

Fuchs, T. 2006. Implicit and explicit temporality. *Philosophy, psychiatry, and psychology* 12(3): 195–98.

Fuchs, T. 2007. The temporal structure of intentionality and its disturbance in schizophrenia. *Psychopathology* 40(4): 229–35.

Fuchs, T. 2013a. The phenomenology of affectivity. In K. W. M. Fulford et al. (eds.), *Oxford handbooks online*. doi: 10.1093/oxfordhb/9780199579563.013.0038.

Fuchs, T. 2013b. Depression, intercorporeality, and interaffectivity. *Journal of consciousness studies* 20(7–8): 219–38.

Gadamer, H. G. 1977. *Philosophical hermeneutics*. Trans. D. Linge. Berkeley: University of California Press.

Gadamer, H. G. 1994. *Truth and method*. Trans. J. Weinsheimer and D. Marshall. New York: Continuum.

Gadamer, H. G. 1996. *The enigma of health*. Trans. J. Gaiger and N. Walker. Stanford, CA: Stanford University Press.

Gallagher, S. 2018. The cure for existential inauthenticity. In K. Aho (ed.), *Existential medicine: Essays on health and illness*. London: Rowman & Littlefield International.

Gerigk, H.-J. 2017. Dostoevsky and Heidegger: Eschatological writer and eschatological thinker. In J. Love (ed.), *Heidegger in Russia and Eastern Europe*. London: Rowman & Littlefield International.

Giddens, A. 1991. *Modernity and self-identity*. Cambridge: Polity Press.

Gilman, C. 1975. *The living of Charlotte Perkins Gilman: An autobiography*. New York: Harper Colophon.

Glenmullen, J. 2001. *Prozac backlash: Overcoming he dangers of Prozac, Zoloft, Paxil, and other antidepressants with safe, effective alternatives*. New York: Simon and Schuster.

Goffman, E. 1963. *Stigma: Notes on the management of spoiled identity*. New York: Touchstone Books.

Gossling, F. G. 1987. *Before Freud: Neurasthenia and the American medical community, 1870–1910*. Urbana: University of Illinois Press.

Groopman, J. 2000. Hurting all over: With so many people in so much pain, how could fibromyalgia not be a disease. *The New Yorker*, November 13.

Groth, M. 2019. Translator's note to Medard Boss: A Memoir. *Existential analysis* 30(1): 169–98.

Guignon, C. 1984. Moods in Heidegger's *Being and Time*. In R. Solomon and C. Calhoun (eds.), *What is an emotion? Classic and contemporary readings*. Oxford: Oxford University Press.

Guignon, C. 1993a. Authenticity, moral values, and psychotherapy. In C. Guignon (ed.), *The Cambridge companion to Heidegger*. Cambridge: Cambridge University Press.

Guignon, C. 1993b. Editor's introduction. In *Dostoevsky's grand inquisitor, with related chapters of the brothers Karamazov*. Indianapolis, IN: Hackett.

Guignon, C. 1999. What is hermeneutics? In B. Fowers, C. Guignon, and F. Richardson, *Re-envisioning psychology: Moral dimensions of theory and practice*. San Francisco: Jossey-Bass.

Guignon, C. 2004. *On being authentic*. New York: Routledge.

Guignon, C. 2011. Heidegger and Kierkegaard on death: Existentiell and the existential. In P. Stokes and A. Buben (eds.), *Kierkegaard and Death*. Bloomington: Indiana University Press.

Hale, N. G. 1995. *The rise and crisis of psychoanalysis in the United States: Freud and the Americans, 1917-1985.* New York: Oxford University Press.

Hall, D. 2001. Ghost in the house. In N. Casey (ed.), *Unholy ghost.* New York: Harper Perennial.

Harris, G. 2006. Proof is scant on psychiatric drug mix for young. *New York Times,* November 23. https://www.nytimes.com/2006/11/23/health/23kids.html?mtrref=www.google.com&gwh=6613C4BC2EF694B89D736F7BC298715D&gwt=pay. Accessed November 20, 2018.

Haugeland, J. 2000. Truth and finitude; Heidegger's transcendental existentialism. In M. Wrathall and J. Malpas (eds.), *Heidegger, authenticity, and modernity: Essays in honor of Hubert L. Dreyfus.* Cambridge, MA: MIT Press.

Haugeland, J. 2013. *Dasein disclosed.* Cambridge, MA: Harvard University Press.

Healy, D. 2006. *Let them eat Prozac: The unhealthy relationship between the pharmaceutical industry and depression.* New York: New York University Press.

Hearn, G. 2009. No clue—what shall we do? Physicians and functional syndromes. *International review of modern sociology* 35: 95–113.

Hickley, P. 2015. Intermittent explosive disorder: The 'illness' that goes on growing. *Behaviorism and mental health.* August 4. http://behaviorismandmentalhealth.com/2015/08/04/intermittent-explosive-disorder-the-illness-that-goes-on-growing/. Accessed December 20, 2018.

Hoffman, P. 1993. Death, time, history: Division II of *Being and Time.* In C. Guignon (ed.), *The Cambridge companion to Heidegger.* Cambridge: Cambridge University Press.

Horwitz, A. 2002. *Creating mental illness.* Chicago: University of Chicago Press.

Horwitz, A., and Wakefield, J. 2007. *The loss of sadness: How psychiatry transformed normal sorrow into depressive disorder.* Oxford: Oxford University Press.

Hosseini, K. 2013. *The kite runner.* New York: Riverhead Books.

Husserl, E. 1970. *The crisis of the European sciences and transcendental phenomenology: An introduction to phenomenological philosophy.* Trans. D. Carr. Evanston, IL: Northwestern University Press.

Husserl, E. 1996. *The phenomenology of internal time consciousness.* Trans. J. Churchill. Bloomington: Indiana University Press.

Ingraham, C. 2015. Nearly 1 in 10 Americans have severe anger issues and access to guns. *Washington Post,* April 8. https://www.washingtonpost.com/news/wonk/wp/2015/04/08/nearly-1-in-10-americans-have-severe-anger-issues-and-access-to-guns/?utm_term=.952e7b5dd41e. Accessed December 18, 2018.

Jaspers, K. 1997. *General psychopathology. Vol. I.* Trans. J. Hoenig and M. W. Hamilton. Baltimore, MD: The Johns Hopkins University Press.

Kaiser, D. 1996. Against biological psychiatry. *Psychiatric Times* 13(2).

Karp, D. 1996. *Speaking of sadness: Depression, disconnection, and the meaning of illness.* Oxford: Oxford University Press.

Karp, D. 2007. *Is it me or my meds: Living with antidepressents.* Cambridge, MA: Harvard University Press.

Kayson, S. 2001. One cheer for melancholy. In N. Casey (ed.), *Unholy ghost.* New York: Harper Perennial.

Khullar, D. 2018. A profusion of diagnoses: That's good and bad. *New York Times,* November 6. https://www.nytimes.com/2018/11/06/well/live/a-profusion-of-diagnoses-thats-good-and-bad.html. Accessed November 11, 2018.

Kierkegaard, S. 1973. *A Kierkegaard Anthology.* Princeton, NJ: Princeton University Press.

Kleinman, A., and Good, B. 1985. *Culture and depression: Studies in the anthropology and the cross-cultural psychiatry of affect and disorder.* Berkeley: University of California Press.

Klerman, G. L. 1990. The patient's right to effective treatment: Implications of Osheroff v. Chestnut Lodge. *American journal of psychiatry* 147: 409–18.

Klerman, G. L. 1991. The Osheroff debate: Finale. *American journal of psychiatry* 148: 387–88.

Knapp, P. C. 1896. Are nervous diseases increasing? *The century* 52.

Kramer, P. 1997. *Listening to Prozac.* New York: Penguin.

Kramer, P. 2011. In defense of antidepressants. *New York Times,* July 10. https://www.nytimes.com/2011/07/10/opinion/sunday/10antidepressants.html?mtrref=www.google.com

&gwh=A567AB659EEB888F32BEEF04C0137080&gwt=pay. Accessed November 25, 2018.

Kutchins, H., and Kirk, S. 1997. *Making us crazy: DSM, the psychiatric bible, and the creation of mental disorders*. New York: Free Press.

Lane, C. 2007. *Shyness: How normal behavior became a sickness*. New Haven, CT: Yale University Press.

Lasch, C. 1978. *The culture of narcissism. American life in an age of diminishing expectations*. New York: W. W. Norton.

Leder, D. 1990. *The absent body*. Chicago, IL: University of Chicago Press.

Levinas, E. 1969. *Totality and infinity: An essay on exteriority*. Trans. A. Lingis. Pittsburgh, PA: Duquesne University Press.

Levine, R. 1997. *Geography of time*. New York: Basic Books.

Levine, R. 2005. A geography of busyness. *Social Research* 72: 355–70.

Lewis, B. 2006. *Moving beyond Prozac, DSM, and the new psychiatry*. Ann Arbor: University of Michigan Press.

Lipowski, Z. 1988. Somatization: The concept and its clinical application. *American journal of psychiatry* 14: 1358–68.

Lown, B. 1999. *The lost art of healing*. New York: Random House.

Marcel, G. 1950. *Mystery of being: Reflection and mystery. Vol. 1*. South Bend, IN: Gateway Editions.

May, P., and Tuma, H. 1964. The effect of psychopathology and Stelazine on length of hospital stay, release rate, and supplemental treatment of schizophrenic patients. *Journal of nervous and mental disease* 139: 362–69.

May, R. 1969. *Love and will*. New York: W. W. Norton.

McDaniel, P. 2003. *Shrinking violets and Caspar milquetoasts: Shyness, power, and intimacy in the United States, 1950-1995*. New York: New York University Press.

McHugh, P. 1999. How psychiatry lost its way. *Commentary* 108: 32–38.

Merleau-Ponty, M. 1962. *Phenomenology of perception*. Trans. C. Smith. New York: Routledge.

Mitchell, A. 2016. Heidegger's breakdown: Health and healing under the care of Dr. V. E. von Gebsattel. *Research in phenomenology* 46: 70–97.

Mogull, S. 2008. Chronology of direct-to-consumer advertising regulation in the United States. *American medical writers association journal* 23(3): 106–9.

Mulhall, S. 2005. Human mortality: Heidegger on how to portray the impossible possibility of Dasein. In H. Dreyfus and M. Wrathall (eds.), *A companion to Heidegger*. Oxford: Blackwell.

Nietzsche. F. 1968. *The will to power*. Trans. W. Kaufmann. New York: Vintage Books.

Nietzsche, F. 2001. *The gay science*. Trans. R. Polt. In C. Guignon and D. Pereboom (eds.), *Existentialism: Basic writings*. Indianapolis, IN: Hackett.

O'Nan, S. 1999. The lost world of Richard Yates: How the great writer of the age of anxiety disappeared from print. *Boston Review*, November/October. Accessed September 1, 2009.

Oldman, J. 2011. The illusions of psychiatry: An exchange. *New York Review of Books*, August 18.

Osnos, E. 2011. Americanitis vs. Chinitis. *The New Yorker*, January 4.

Paris, B. 2008. *Dostoevsky's greatest characters: A new approach to "notes from the underground," crime and punishment, and the brothers Karamazov*. New York: Palgrave Macmillan.

Piguet, C. et al. 2009. Phenomenology of racing and crowded thoughts in mood disorders: A theoretical appraisal. *Journal of affective disorders*. https://doi.org/10.1016/j.Jad.2009 .05.006.

Ratcliffe, M. 2008. *Feelings of being: Phenomenology, psychiatry, and the sense of reality*. Oxford: Oxford University Press.

Ratcliffe, M. 2013. Why mood matters. In M. Wrathall (ed.), *The Cambridge companion to Being and Time*. Cambridge: Cambridge University Press, 157–76.

Ratcliffe, M. 2015. *Experiences of depression: A study in phenomenology*. Oxford: Oxford University Press.

Ratcliffe, M. 2017. Selfhood, schizophrenia, and the interpersonal regulation of experience. In C. Durt et al. (eds.), *Embodiment, enaction, and culture: Investigating the constitution of the shared world*. Cambridge, MA: MIT Press.

Ratcliffe, M., and Broome, M. 2012. Existential phenomenology in psychiatric illness. In S. Crowell (ed.), *The Cambridge companion to existentialism*. Cambridge: Cambridge University Press.

Ratcliffe, M., Ruddell, M., and Smith, B. 2014. What is a 'sense of foreshortened future?' A phenomenological study of trauma, trust, and time. *Frontiers in psychology* 5: 1016. https://doi.org/10.3389/fpsyg.2014.01026.

Rettew, D. 2000. Avoidant personality disorder, generalized social phobia, and shyness: Putting the personality back into personality disorders. *Harvard review of psychiatry* 8(6): 283–97.

Ricoeur, P. 1981. *Hermeneutics and the human sciences*. Trans. J. Thompson. Cambridge: Cambridge University Press.

Richardson, F. 2012. Psychology and virtue ethics. *Journal of theoretical and philosophical psychology* 32(1): 24–34.

Rose, N. 2003. Neurochemical selves. *Society*, November/December: 46–59.

Rose, N. 2007. *The politics of life itself: Biomedicine, power, and subjectivity in the twenty-first century*. Princeton, NJ: Princeton University Press.

Rosenberg, R. 2013. Abnormal is the new normal. *Slate*. http://www.slate.com/articles/health_and_science/medical_examiner/2013/04/diagnostic_and_statistical_manual_fifth_edition_why_will_half_the_u_s_population.html. Accessed on July 30, 2018.

Safranski, R. 1998. *Martin Heidegger: Between good and evil*. Trans. E. Osers. Cambridge: Cambridge University Press.

Sartre, J. P. 1956. *Being and nothingness: An essay in phenomenological ontology*. Trans. H. Barnes. Secaucus, NJ: The Citadel Press.

Sartre, J. P. 2001. The humanism of existentialism. In C. Guignon and D. Pereboom (eds.), *Existentialism: Basic writings*. Indianapolis, IN: Hackett.

Sass, L., and Parnas, J. 2007. Explaining schizophrenia: the relevance of phenomenology. In M. C. Chung, K. W. M Fulford, and G. Graham (eds.), *International perspectives in philosophy and psychiatry: Reconceiving schizophrenia*. New York: Oxford University Press.

Schmid, U. 2011. Heidegger and Dostoevsky: Philosophy and politics. *Dostoevsky studies* 15: 37–45.

Schultz, D., and Flasher, L. 2011. Charles Taylor, phronesis, and medicine: Ethics and interpretation in illness narrative. *Journal of medicine and philosophy* 36: 394–409.

Schuster, S. 2017. 33 subtle ways anxiety affects your daily life. *The mighty*. Retrieved from https://themighty.com/2017/01/how-anxiety-affects-daily-life/.

Scott, S. 2005. The red, shaking fool: Dramaturgical dilemmas in shyness. *Symbolic interaction* 28(1): 91–110.

Scott, S. 2006. The medicalization of shyness: From social misfits to social fitness. *Sociology of health and illness* 28(2): 133–53.

Shenk, J. W. 2001. A melancholy of mine own. In N. Casey (ed.), *Unholy ghost*. New York: Harper Perennial.

Shorter, E. 1996. *A history of psychiatry: From the era of the asylum to the age of Prozac*. New York: John Wiley and Sons.

Showalter, E. 1985. *The female malady: Women, madness and English cultures, 1830-1980*. New York: Pantheon Books.

Shuster. D. 2011. *Neurasthenic nation: America's search for health, happiness, and comfort, 1869-1920*. New Brunswick, NJ: Rutgers University Press.

Simmel, G. 1997. The metropolis and mental life. In D. Frisby and M. Featherstone (eds.), *Simmel on culture*. London: Sage.

Sinaikin, P. 2010. *Psychiatryland: How to protect yourself from pill-pushing psychiatrists and develop a personal plan for optimal mental health*. New York: iUniverse.

Smith, P. 1988. *Discerning the subject*. Minneapolis: University of Minnesota Press.

Solomon, A. 2001. *The noonday demon: An atlas of depression*. New York: Simon and Schuster.

Spanbaeur, T. 2013. *I love you more*. Portland: Hawthorne Books.

Spiegel, A. 2005. The dictionary of disorder. *The New Yorker*, January, 56–63.

Stanghellini, G., and Rosfort, R. 2013. *Emotions and personhood: Exploring fragility—making sense of vulnerability*. Oxford: Oxford University Press.

Stenke, D. 2001. Poodle bed. In N. Casey (ed.), *Unholy ghost*. New York: Harper Perennial.

Stossel, S. 2015. *My age of anxiety: Fear, hope, dread, and the search for peace of mind*. New York: Vintage Books.

Styron, W. 1990. *Darkness visible: A memoir of madness*. New York: Modern Library.

Surgeon General. 1999. *Mental health: A report of the surgeon general*. http://surgeongeneral.gov/library/mentalhealth/chapter2/sec3.html. Accessed September 20, 2018.

Svenaeus, F. 2000. *The hermeneutic of medicine and the phenomenology of health: Steps towards a philosophy of medical practice*. Dordrecht: Kluwer.

Svenaeus, F. 2007. Do antidepressants affect the self? A phenomenological approach. *Medicine, healthcare and philosophy* 10: 153–66.

Svenaeus, F. 2011. Illness as unhomelike being-in-the-world: Heidegger and the phenomenology of medicine. *Medicine, healthcare and philosophy* 14(3): 333–43.

Szasz, T. 1961. *The myth of mental illness*. New York: Harper and Row.

Szasz. T. 2007. *The medicalization of everyday life*. Syracuse, NY: Syracuse University Press.

Talbot, M. 2001. The shyness syndrome. *New York Times Sunday Magazine*, June.

Taylor, C. 1985. *Human agency and language: Philosophical papers. Vol. 1*. Cambridge: Cambridge University Press.

Taylor, C. 2007. *The secular age*. Cambridge, MA: Harvard University Press.

Thomson, I. 2013. Death and demise in *Being and Time*. In M. Wrathall (ed.), *The Cambridge companion to Heidegger's* Being and Time. Cambridge: Cambridge University Press.

Tolstoy, L. 1994. *My confession, my religion*. Trans. I. Hapgood. Midland, MI: Avensblume Press.

Trawny, P. 2018. Thinking-time: Or, why do 'we' ask about the future of Heidegger's thinking. In R. Polt and G. Fried (eds.), *After Heidegger*. London: Rowman & Littlefield International.

Ulmer, D. K., and Schwartzburd, L. 1996. Treatment of time pathologies. *Heart and mind: the practice of cardiac psychology*. Washington DC: American Psychological Association.

Van Der Kolk, B. 2014. *The body keeps score: Brain, mind, and body in the healing of trauma*. New York: Penguin Books.

Vedantam, S. 2006. Experts defining mental disorders are linked to drug firms. *Washington Post*, April 19. http://www.washingtonpost.com/wpdyn/content/article/2006/04/19/AR2006041902560.html?noredirect=on. Accessed November 15, 2018.

Wallace, D. F. 2004. *Oblivion: Stories*. New York: Little, Brown and Company.

Wallace, D. F. 2006. *Consider the lobster: And other essays*. New York: Little, Brown and Company.

Weber, M. 1998. *The Protestant ethic and the spirit of capitalism*. Trans. T. Parsons. Los Angeles, CA: Roxbury Publishing Company.

Wessely, S. 1990. Old wine in new bottles: Neursathenia and 'Me.' *Psychological medicine* 20: 35–53.

White, C. 2005. *Time and death: Heidegger's analysis of finitude*. London: Ashgate.

Wrathall, M. 2001. Background practices, capacities, and Heideggerian disclosure. In M. Wrathall and J. Malpas (eds.), *Heidegger, coping, and cognitive science: A Festschrift for Hubert Dreyfus. Vol. 2*. Cambridge, MA: MIT Press.

Wurtzel, E. 1995. *Prozac nation: Young and depressed in America*. New York: Riverhead Books.

Wyatt, R. 1985. Science and psychiatry. In H. Kaplan and B. Sadock (eds.), *Comprehensive textbook of psychiatry*. Baltimore, MD: Williams and Wilkins.

Young, R. 2003. Patients like Linda. *Journal of the American medical association* 290(2): 165–66.

Index

Made in the USA
Coppell, TX
03 June 2021